This work is dedicated to my parents who each served in WWII before I was born. Semper Fi to you both.

Gunnery SGT Roger C Campbell, USMC, Aerial Combat Photographer. He enlisted immediately after Pearl Harbor was attacked and served in the South Pacific until coming back to the U.S. in 1944 with malaria.

WAVE Pharmacist's Mate Satanik (Nikki)Vartanian. She served with distinction at the San Diego Naval Hospital during WWII in a variety of roles.

They met and married and I was born in 1945. None of this would have been possible without either of you.

To My Readers…

The Vietnam Veterans Memorial tour was not limited to the ten months I spent on the road actually doing it, but rather is the culmination of a series of events spanning more than twenty years, seemingly trivial and unrelated, sometimes annoying but always instructive and necessary.

I think it is important to let you know where I was before I can tell you where I've been. None of us lives in a vacuum: every decision, every turn we make and direction we follow has consequences and repercussions; some you feel right away and others that need to percolate for a time.

So it begins.

Out of the Ashes

Out of the Ashes

A Vietnam Veteran's Journey
Among the Tombstones of His Generation

Bruce Campbell

**Out of the Ashes: A Viet Nam Veteran's Journey
among the Tombstones of His Generation**
Published by Vet Media Co
Boulder, CO

Campbell, Bruce A./ Author
Out of the Ashes: A Viet Nam Veteran's Journey
among the Tombstones of His Generation
Bruce A. Campbell

ISBN: 978-1516979318

PERSONAL MEMOIRS

Cover photo by author. Vietnam veteran's memorial outside the Haywood County Courthouse, Waynesville, North Carolina

QUANTITY PURCHASES: Schools, companies, professional groups, clubs, and other organizations may qualify for special terms when ordering quantities of this title. For information, email bcampbell@vetmediaco.net.

PUBLISHED BY

VET MEDIA

Denver, CO

"Empathy is really the opposite of spiritual meanness. It's the capacity to understand that every war is both won and lost. And that someone else's pain is as meaningful as your own."

- Barbara Kingsolver

1. Why?

This is the most commonly asked question I get, and after three years of planning and nearly a year on the road, I'm still not sure how to give a straightforward answer as it seems to change or evolve over time.

My immediate family thought I was nuts, just straight out bat-spit crazy for doing the Tour. My cousins couldn't believe I would or could spend a year out of my life doing something as bizarre as this.

Just so you know, in my family I was the first of my generation, the only male among my sister and first cousins, and the only one that was called to Vietnam…the rest all saw what they saw or heard what they heard through the media of the day.

My friends thought the Tour was something cool to do; something different, and that it would be a kind of adventure. I think many of them looked at it as an extended vacation.

Life at the moment of decision was very open and kind of pointless at the same time. I had just shut down my second company in five years and really had nothing better to do than contemplate that I had to be somewhere, doing something, each day, and it didn't have to be in Denver.

A little background. In 2008, when Wall Street imploded and after nearly 20 years in the mortgage business, I was forced to close my company. In 2009 I teamed up with my best friend Preston to open a bicycle shop, thinking it would be a good way to spend my remaining working years. I would be sales/management and he would be service and repair. After a little more than 2 years he died, and without that arm of the company producing revenue I could not keep it going.

About the same time, I was given an opportunity through my church of attending a five day workshop on a new way of dealing with PTSD and other hypersensitivity issues, with an eye toward veterans returning from the Gulf Wars. During the workshop the idea of this tour came fully born out of my imagination in a way that I just couldn't ignore. If you've ever been hit by a cosmic 2x4 you will likely understand. The idea was a gift from something outside myself and so outrageous that I had to give it some consideration. One thing I have learned after nearly 10 years on a serious spiritual journey is this: when the universe calls, pay attention.

Over the previous twenty years I had gotten used to seeking out Vietnam Veterans memorials when I traveled, and by the time of the workshop I had already seen perhaps thirty memorials in several different states.

And after the idea took root, I figured, okay, how many more could there be to see? Forty or fifty? When I finally stopped researching about a year and a half later I had more than 750 in my database, in 49 states, and would find more almost by accident as people around the country became aware of my project through social media and passed information along to me.

When I left home on Day One, May 31, 2013, the list had 785 memorials, most confirmed, some speculative, to visit and I *would* see each and every one of them.

2. My History

I grew up in Southern California during a pretty peaceful time. From the time my father returned home from Korea in 1952 when I was 6, to my high school days, there didn't seem to be a lot happening in the world, at least nothing that caught my attention. We moved to Culver City, a small city of about 33,000 and completely surrounded by Los Angeles, but totally self-sustaining with its own police and fire departments and an independent school system.

Life was pretty easy, and I graduated in 1963, a decent but lackadaisical student, and went off to college where I flamed out after only three semesters. By then, Vietnam was all over everything and it was clear that it would be sucking up a lot of draft-eligible young men.

I was 19 and adrift, so I took the plunge and enlisted. Unwilling to tell my dad that I had flunked out of college, I instead let him know that I had just joined the U.S. Navy. As a former Marine in both WWII and Korea, I'm sure after the initial shock, he was both proud that I was continuing the family tradition of serving, and I was at least smart enough to stay out of the Army or Marine Corps.

One of my motivations was to avoid Vietnam with all dispatch. The Navy, in spite of being involved at the start (The Gulf of Tonkin incident in 1964) had a very small presence in country at the time.

My friends at the time, principally Gary, Kenny and John, all decided to wait it out and take their chances. All three of them wound up being drafted. Kenny served stateside while Gary and John both spent their time in Germany, and I wound up in Vietnam anyway. So much for planning and logic.

After Boot Camp in San Diego and Class A Technical School outside Chicago, I was ordered to report to a Destroyer, the USS Damato, DD871, in Norfolk, VA. That would be my home from October of 1965 till my discharge in February of 1969. I was only there for three and a half years, but it seemed longer. Rated a Machinist's Mate, my duty station was the engine room. If anyone was ever less suited to being a mechanic, I would be hard pressed to know who it could be. Nevertheless, the needs of the service dictate, and that day they needed another machinist's mate.

Among the first things that occur upon enlistment is the taking of the Basic Battery Test, the military's way of evaluating your basic knowledge as a way of assigning you a rating. I was good at taking the kind of test that was administered. My scores were nearly perfect across the board with the lowest score higher than many recruits' highest score. And, of course, my lowest score was in mechanical aptitude. Not the most logical scenario for a newly minted Machinist Mate.

The Navy had its benefits. The next year we spent about six months sailing the Mediterranean Sea, visiting virtually every country in southern Europe, and some in the Middle East and North Africa. I remember Beirut when it was still a vibrant and beautiful city. I can remember going to a movie theater in Sfax, Tunisia and watching a John Wayne film dubbed in French and subtitled in Arabic. The Duke speaking French?

I remember a cruise to Finale Ligure on the Italian Riviera. Our ship was named for an Italian-American soldier originally from this small coastal town. The city welcomed us with open arms, laying out a really, really long red carpet across the entire beach for us to walk over on our way to the town, and, oh, how they honored us during our brief stay.

Naval vessels have criteria for being named. Aircraft Carriers carry the names of famous admirals, politicians, or notable presidents. Battleships are named after states, cruisers after major cities, submarines after fish and marine mammals, and destroyers after deceased Medal of Honor recipients. Other classes of support ships are similarly grouped. Oilers (refueling ships) are named after rivers with native American names, ammunition ships after volcanoes, and hospital ships after virtues such as mercy or comfort. There are historical exceptions to all classes but, as a general rule, the criteria stand.

In 1968 we were assigned to a task group that cruised completely around South America, creating another whole flock of memories.

But 1967 was the year we were sent to Vietnam. Understand that not only was the navy not hugely invested in the war outside of the riverine patrols, but east coast ships were usually an afterthought when you consider the ships assigned to the west coast and Hawaii. So we were pretty surprised at having to go. Tours were limited to a year for Army, Navy and Air Force (thirteen and a half months for the Marines for some unaccountable reason), and we spent nearly five of those twelve months in transit, with only seven months of actual combat time remaining.

We served. We stood watch after watch, went to battle stations several times a day. Shot at "them" from a distance of several miles while they shot back at us, hitting us twice and causing some serious onboard damage. Altogether we had one Purple Heart awarded from combat and one non-combat death among our crew in the area of operations. I've seen Jeff's name on The Wall in Washington DC three times, twice on traveling walls and once at the Navy Memorial on the grounds of Coronado Naval Station in San Diego.

With all respect to the boots on the ground, well-deserved I might add, I know our service at sea was not nearly as intrusive to body and soul as service *In Country*, but it did have its own levels of stress and did take a toll on all of us over time. I commend my brothers and sisters in service at the time for their efforts and sacrifice, whatever their assigned specialty, in spite of the way the war was administered, which is a conversation for another time.

We arrived back in the States in January of 1968. I immediately took leave to go home before flying back to meet the ship on its arrival in Norfolk later that month.

February 18th of 1969, another year and another major cruise behind me, I packed my sea bag, got my papers and said goodbye to that part of my life. I was 23.

3. Free at Last

For better or for worse, I spent a lot of time trying to catch up. I was back in L.A. having missed the Summer of Love and all that created the Zeitgeist for my generation. I let my hair and beard grow, moved to Beverly Hills into my first apartment, a bachelor pad with a small fridge and hot plate for the grand sum of $95 a month. But it was mine.

I conveniently "forgot" about the service and Vietnam, and lived a free and easy life for a long time, cruising from one job to another and generally enjoying myself. I went back to school after nearly 10 years, doing much better than the last time but enjoying it less. Eventually I left again, halfway through my senior year, on my own terms. A diploma just didn't seem that important any more.

> *From 1969 through roughly 1979 I spent time doing sheet metal work, driving a big rig truck, selling women's hairpieces on the street, stocking super-market shelves in the middle of the night, selling wine, teaching courses for a local open university, commercial diving, writing a column for a Marina del Rey magazine, selling and managing real estate, coaching women's softball, skiing and scuba diving for pleasure, and other pursuits.*

The entire decade of the '70's I was living in and on Venice Beach, California, spending part of almost every day on the beach; there was something soothing and relaxing about the water. It was a time when people were freer about themselves and their actions than at any time before or since. I joke from time to time that you could have not one but two whole relationships, from beginning to end, in the span of a one-day garage sale on the beach. What a life!

Then it turned dark.

From 1977 through 1980 I worked for a real estate firm in the Marina area, primarily in property management. In 1980, feeling hip beyond words, I willingly fell victim to the popularity of drugs in the new culture of the day for a very short but very impactful time. It cost me everything…my job, my money, all my friends who were still doing, and I had to leave everything behind and start over. It was painful.

I moved to the San Fernando Valley and went to work for my sister and brother-in-law at their quick print business. My brother in law, Ron, was probably the hardest worker I ever knew. He quickly turned a failing business into a huge success. I was lucky that it wasn't exactly rocket science and I was able to hit the ground running, clean and sober and grateful for the chance. I cruised right through the '80's like a real citizen with a condo, a Mercedes and the other accoutrements of modern life. My military past was buried very deeply, even less than an afterthought at that point, but it was about to change.

Right around 1990 during a night out, my date and I rented a recent Bruce Willis movie that came out the year before but neither of us had ever heard of: *In Country*. Being fans of Willis we took it home and watched it. The movie is about Uncle Emmett, a returned Vietnam vet, someone about 90% able to maintain life in rural Kentucky with assistance from his niece from time to time. His brother/her father was killed in Vietnam before her birth. She finds a stash of letters from him to her mother before he died and now wants to know what it was like over there. Emmett doesn't want to talk about it. It ends at The Wall, which was still fairly new at the time. It was in indelible experience. Perhaps less than a cosmic 2x4, but powerful enough to make me sit up and take notice.

The Wall is something I knew about but paid no attention to, as I was still holding the whole military "thing" way out to the side. Till the moment it appeared onscreen I hadn't seen a drawing or picture of it that I could recall. Seeing it in the film for the first time, I resolved in the moment that I would visit The Wall as soon as possible.

I want to take a moment and tell you about the book. The movie In Country is from the book of the same name written by Bobbie Ann Mason. I immediately bought the book and devoured it. It rang so authentic and from such a personal place that I started imagining her actually being from a family that lost a son/brother/father/ uncle in the war. Perhaps she was the daughter coming to terms with the loss of a father.

Much later I was able to meet her on a book tour through Denver for her latest release, and took the opportunity to ask her about it. "No, it is just a story I came up with. I'm from Kentucky and write about Kentucky people," she said. I was crushed.

It...was...so...real. I have since come to understand that information comes to us from very unexpected sources and at seemingly random times, and the fact that it was fiction makes it no less real to the heart; that divine truths have always inspired and at the level of the soul they are always true. This idea became something that would ring even more true after my visit to the Vietnam Veterans memorial in Rochester, NY, a subject for another chapter.

At the time, I had left the family business and was working for a mortgage company in the San Fernando Valley. In an illustration of how "timing is everything," almost immediately after I saw the movie, the owners of the company announced a contest. First prize was a trip anywhere in the country the winner wanted to go, all expenses paid. All I needed to do was beat out all the other loan officers in production for the month.

I won, and less than 60 days from seeing In Country, I was winging my way east to visit The Wall. Funny how the universe works when you set the right intention.

4. *The Wall*

During my three plus years in Norfolk, I made the Dulles to LAX round trip two or three times each year, but this was my first time going the other way. I was excited. This was no luxury flight, and my budget was Motel 6 all the way, but it was still an adventure. Got there, got to bed and got up the next morning ready to see what, till recently, I wasn't even willing to acknowledge.

It was wet and drizzly. It was cold. It was not great weather for someone planning to be on foot most of the day without an umbrella. But I kept on. Walking through the park, I waded through immense puddles on the low lying strip of concrete guiding me to my destination. I kept up a watch, waiting for my first glimpse.

I had been warned that the memorial was hard to spot unless you are right there upon it, then it was impossible to take your eyes off it. All too true.

There were only a few people at the memorial that day. It was early, the weather was questionable and it wasn't nearly the attraction that it has since become. But those wonderful people from the National Park Service, the ones charged with the day to day of the memorial, were on duty and incredibly helpful.

I had four names on my list to find and pay my respects to: Cliff Volke, a high school friend, one year behind me, who survived his first tour In Country but not the second; Jeff Brown, the shipmate who was killed in an unfortunate shipboard accident; and Mike Uhlig, my first year college roommate. The fourth was another shipmate who I had heard was ordered back to Vietnam for riverine duty and was killed, but his name wasn't there, so I guess it was just a rumor. God knows there were a lot of them in those days.

Amazingly, as soon as I arrived at the memorial the sky began clearing. The drizzle stopped and the clouds thinned enough that the day brightened.

The wet stone of The Wall fairly glowed from within and reflected everything. I was spellbound by the experience. Searching and finding, I was able to locate all three names and did the rubbings that have become so popular at memorials all around the country.

Suddenly, I was overwhelmed and needed to sit down. The only place to sit was on the berm guarding the front of the wall, elevated a few inches above the sidewalk. So I rested for a few minutes, my butt on the berm and my back against the cool, damp marble, and let my mind try to process this experience.

About three hours later I felt a tug on my jacket sleeve. It was one of the female Park Service officers who had apparently been eyeing the situation and finally got a little concerned about me, sitting there, crying, immobile. She got me to my feet and we started walking, first along one side of the wall, then the other for what seemed like an hour but was likely only 15 minutes or so…talking to me…walking me back from a really bad place.

It couldn't have been easy. Physically a big guy, not only am I a load to have to push and pull around, but this was before the digital age when all the names were on paper in a book larger than Webster's Unabridged Dictionary. With me in one hand and that big book in the other she kept it real, kept it moving and got me back into the world once again. She was/is one of the absolutely real angels I have been privileged to cross paths with in this life.

As soon as she felt comfortable, she let me go my own way. As soon as I turned the corner and headed back the way I had come, the clouds closed in once again and the drizzle returned, stronger than before. I had been blessed that day.

Things have changed since then. While at The Wall this time I noticed a number of things. There were more exhibits surrounding The Wall than before...less open space. The site is somewhat more regimented in terms of access and egress, and there were more visitors to The Wall than I would have ever imagined. Thanks to technology, the park service people overseeing the memorial now have hand-held digital readers much smaller and lighter than the old paper directory, making it much easier to answer questions and guide people to the name they are interested in. I have huge respect for these people who, day in and day out, witness off the chart emotion and deal with it effortlessly and respectfully.

5. Reunion

While the Los Angeles/Washington, DC leg of the journey was non-stop, I detoured through Kentucky on the way back for a visit with my old friend and shipmate Joe Fischer. Joe is a former New Yorker living at this time in Lexington with his wife Barbara, and working for Procter & Gamble. I had seen Joe a couple of times in California back in the '70's and had met his wife once before. It had been a long, long time between contacts.

Joe was without a doubt my closest friend aboard the DAMATO for almost the entire time I was aboard ship. We traveled together, got drunk together, and explored the seamier side of several cities around the world together.

> *I can still remember the two of us flying from San Francisco to L.A. for a wild weekend, staying at my mom's house during those few hours we actually slept, and partying so late the last night that we missed our flight to San Diego and were in danger of being AWOL the next morning.*
> *My mother browbeat my dad to drive us, between three and six a.m., from L.A. to San Diego.*
> *We got back aboard just in time to cast off for South America. It would have meant a world of hurt had we been even 15 minutes later.*

It was a great couple of days exploring parts of Kentucky and Southern Ohio, eating some regional delights and catching up. Like me, he had done his four years and got out, only to re-up and serve out his 20 years ending as a Chief Petty Officer. Machinery always came much easier to him than to me.

One of the cities we drove through was Frankfort, the capitol of Kentucky and the site of my second memorial visit. Unfortunately, after seeing The Wall just a couple days before, the one in Frankfort seemed interesting but hardly as spectacular. I have since come to understand just how special and significant it really is.

The one thing that the memorial in Frankfort did accomplish is to inspire me to seek out other memorials in my future travels...the next nudge in a chain of events that led me to do this "Tour."

Twenty some years later and in another state entirely, I was able to reconnect with Joe and Barbara once again during the Tour. They are still together, thriving in retirement, and she's still cute as a button. Way to go, Joe.

2. The Game

The next push came about in a very unexpected way. I was living in a condo in Encino, California when an interesting couple purchased a unit at the opposite end of the building. Antonio Fargas and his wife, Sandy, were my new neighbors. Those of you who were fans of late '70's cop dramas will remember Antonio as Huggy Bear, a pivotal character in the television series *Starsky and Hutch*.

They hosted a regular Friday night poker party in their home. One night several months after they moved in, and after getting to know them a little, a seat opened up and I was asked to sit in on "The Game." I never gave up the seat till I actually left California for Colorado for good. Those were some of the best Friday nights of my life.

The games bore little actual relationship to poker. All the players loved wild cards and split pots, the kind of games where five aces guaranteed you only a share of the pot and sometimes the lowest hand took away the most money. It kept the money flowing, everyone in till the last card on almost every hand, and the conversation never stopped.

Among the other players were Ted Lange (Isaac from *The Love Boat*), Richard Gant (*Men of a Certain Age*), and Tucker Smallwood (*Contact* and *Space, Above and Beyond*). Tucker is a Vietnam veteran; a Special Forces officer with stories that had me riveted from time to time.

We talked and shared our experiences…mine weren't nearly as impactful as his, especially the one about his re-birth day, September 14th, when he was wounded, should have bled out, actually flatlined in surgery, but survived, and has gone on to a more than four-decade career as an actor.

Tucker and Antonio have remained my good friends. Antonio and Sandy have moved to Las Vegas, and he still works and thrives as a result of his history as Huggy Bear, a character that has morphed into a cultural icon. I always try to arrange a visit with them whenever I happen to pass through Vegas.

Tucker still lives in L.A., is more or less retired, at least on paper, and continues to participate in local theater, writing and performing his poetry, playing golf and thoroughly enjoying life; a far cry from the soldier lying torn and bleeding his life out halfway around the world.

He also participates and advocates for veterans at every opportunity by writing articles for veterans-centric publications, doing speaking engagements and serving on the boards of veteran non-profits. He is an inspiration to me, and one of those mental yardsticks that let me know I have not done enough and could do more.

Recently, Tucker posted on Facebook a response to an uninformed posting on PTSD. It highlights the difficulty the general public has in understanding PTSD and its effect on society in the telling of his own story.
He has given me permission to print it here:

Yesterday an article was posted here by shock jock Mark Savage, mocking PTSD and soldiers who seek treatment and compensation. Savage is a very well paid shill for the Right. He has an agenda and an opinion. Some commented, "He's never served, he has no right to criticize."

Civilians have a right to an opinion. As do veterans, including combat veterans. Opinions are like assholes; everybody has one. Opinions are not facts. PTSD has been recognized, comparatively recently as an enduring emotional trauma caused by combat, violent crime, accidents, any number of serious life events.

It's not new, only the identification of it is. I can't say whether patrols in Fallujah were any more stressful than Normandy or Pusan or Ia Drang Valley…but for some soldiers, it was life-altering. Period. You might walk thru the same operation that causes me nightmares for years. What's your point? I'll now recount for you my journey.

In 2010, I was persuaded by friends to file for PTSD. When I resisted, they told me to donate the money if that made me feel better. but the statistics were needed to justify funding. I filed. A year later I received an evaluation appointment. I requested documentation from the two therapists that had treated me, both eminent in the field. I'd been diagnosed and began treatment in 1988.
I began medication in 2006. None of the statements had been read by my evaluator. He knew nothing of combat or my history and his manner was simply bizarre. He would repeat my responses back, distorted, purposefully misunderstood. He was curt, dismissive. And I eventually realized his entire intention was to make me lose control, to become angry. Months later my claim was denied. I then did become angry.

I filed a request for re-evaluation. More months later, I was seen by a second VA representative. He had read my history, my treatment, my evaluations. A total of 30 months passed, from start to finish, 43 years after coming home from war, when the US Army finally acknowledged that my experiences in combat had created enduring emotional trauma in my life. THAT was really all I sought and it was personally satisfying to finally have it.

Conditions vary from veteran to veteran. For some it is a nuisance; for others it is debilitating. Impossible to keep a family together, keep a home, keep a job, sleep in peace. Mental illness is an enigma to the more fortunate. But to politicize care and treatment for damaged veterans is contemptible, beyond forgiveness and I regard my mission to advocate for treatment as a sacred calling.

7. Other Factors

Giving you chapter and verse of all the winks, nudges, pushes and body blows along the way that led me to do the Tour would use up a lot of unnecessary paper. To abbreviate the process, here is a short list of some of the ways the veteran experience has crept into my consciousness:

Innumerable hours spent at the VA: You are a literal captive to the process and can't help but notice things and people around you; the air of infirmity and hopelessness, the sense of a lack of any real caring, knowing you are but an output of this giant medical "factory." You look around and admit to yourself, "There but for the grace of god go I," and feel immediately ashamed of your judgment, and start to wonder, is there anything I can do?

Parking at the Denver VA is a zoo. Both the parking structure and the limited footprint of the facility leave it always crowded. There are lots of meters to feed and, since everything takes longer than you expect, the meters frequently expire and tickets are given out. I would frequently empty my pockets of change feeding expired meters, hoping to avoid misery placed upon misery.

Occasionally a veteran would ask for a ride home, not wanting to wait for their free van. We are all brothers so, why not? I got to hear some of their stories along the way, and they all took root in my subconscious.

Denver is home to a lot of parades, and the annual Veterans Day parade is one of the largest. I was a spectator for several years before actually joining the parade one year with my Legion Post. There are a lot of dedicated veterans who are always willing to take part and help in any way they can.

Visits to other memorials: In the years leading up to the tour I visited memorials in several states in the course of my normal travel. Whether large (Angel Fire, New Mexico) or small (downtown Los Angeles) they all imparted a sense of duty, of passion and pride in accomplishment, however ephemeral, and the experiences stayed with me

Joining and giving back: After a very long time without actually affiliating myself, I joined the American Legion, Veterans of Foreign Wars and the Vietnam Veterans of America. It brought me into direct contact with more veterans, more stories, more opportunities to help, and more to add to what was swirling around in my head.

I was suddenly more conscious of stories in the media about veterans and the trials and challenges many of them face...another nudge in the direction my own consciousness was heading.

I took off my virtual blinders and noticed the homeless in every big city wearing camo and OD jackets and other castoff clothing of military origin. I know at least some of them were genuine vets, but were too proud to ask for help from agencies tasked to give them assistance, too afflicted to understand what it was they needed or just out of hope for a better outcome.

I paid attention to the music that came out of the Vietnam experience. Two of my favorites are "Still in Saigon" by the Charlie Daniels Band, a story of a returned vet suffering from PTSD and not knowing how to deal with it; and "After the War" by a Denver friend of mine, Timothy P Irvin, about a veteran going to The Wall in DC to face up to a past he hoped he had left behind, only to be rocked to his core by a discovery he makes on The Wall

But there was one big experience that put it all into focus for me: Human Software Engineering.

* * * * *

I am a licensed Practitioner of Religious Science, a metaphysical faith path, that allows me access and opportunity to attend classes and workshops not available to the general public. One of these opportunities was an incredible five-day workshop dealing with PTSD and other hypersensitivity issues, tailored to returning Gulf War Veterans, but applicable to veterans of all vintages as well as anyone dealing with deeply held trauma in their lives.

The program was run by Tom Stone, a remarkable man with an incredibly varied CV. Human Software Engineering is the term he coined for his work: essentially a way to debug the mind, at its core a giant computer, of unwanted and intrusive mental malware, a technique that enables you to remove the emotional context of an event without wiping out the memory of the event.

I've seen the result. One of the other participants in the workshop was a veteran of the First Gulf War. He was temporarily absent from his duty station one day when the post was destroyed by enemy action. He was the only survivor of his unit.

He had not been able to sleep through the night since it happened, waking at the slightest sound, and unable to hear loud noises of any kind without becoming instantly and, sometimes dangerously, defensive. After a session with Tom he was able to sleep well for the first time since his deployment.

Somewhere along the way in this workshop, all of my experiences involving the military, veterans and memorials came together: An opportunity to travel, to support other veterans, and further my spiritual journey and do some good in the world.

8. Decision Time

Okay...the project is a GO: visit, record and pray over every Vietnam-specific Veterans' memorial in the country. No biggie.

To date I had seen The Wall in Washington DC, a wall in Venice Beach, California, Memorials in Colorado, Kentucky, New Mexico, California, Utah, Arizona and Kansas/Missouri. I guessed I would eventually find somewhere between fifty and seventy-five more here and there. The joke was really on me as, a year and a half later, my research stopped at 785. I can't know if it was comprehensive, but the database had memorials in 49 states... all but Alaska. Big Gulp.

Oh well. Roll up your sleeves and get to work planning, I told myself. Of course now, I had the time to do it.

The story wouldn't be complete however, without an understanding of some other life events, different from those in the previous chapter, which brought me to this project in the first place. Briefly reviewing the last several years...

The early and mid-2000's saw me flying high, doing a great business with my mortgage company. I had caught the internet mortgage origination wave early: web-savvy people seeking loans on-line in great numbers for the first time, and everything was clicking.

In the nearly 20 years I had spent in the business up to that time, there had been a number of boom and bust cycles, and this was a boom for certain. I was working with some good people, doing good work for deserving people and investing well. Or so I thought. In the mid 2000's I started buying property in Colorado and Nevada...my retirement looked solid. Then, 2008 came along and my world just fell off a cliff.

This was a bust like no other I had been through. Property values plummeted (like immediately after the great California earthquake of 1994), interest rates soared (as in the Jimmy Carter administration). But, the real difference was the numbers of lenders exiting the business, just shutting their doors one after another, leaving nothing behind but dust and ashes. The industry just burned to the ground. I had to close the doors of my company after nearly thirteen years.

All of the property I had acquired along the way, which had been operating at a slight loss, fell like dominoes when the income stopped cold. It felt like the dark ages settling around my shoulders...the next three years felt like three hundred.

An opportunity came along to open a bicycle shop. This had been on my wish list for decades. I love to bicycle and had been on big bike events in California and Mexico in the past. But these were not ordinary bicycles.

Electric bicycles had been around for about 20 years or so and had become very popular in Europe and essential in China, with millions on the road every day. And technology had been making them lighter, faster and less expensive over time.

My best friend Preston came to work with me...he could fix anything, and while I handled most of the business and sales functions, he puttered happily in the repair and maintenance arena. We struggled through two and a half years of steady, if sluggish sales. We started seeing some daylight at the end of this particular tunnel when, in October of 2010, he had a massive stroke and passed away two days later. Needing his expertise to stay afloat and lacking the resources to hire anyone else, those doors closed as well, and I was well and truly retired. Again... I needed something to do.

Two months later I enrolled in the Human Software Engineering workshop and the rest, as they say, is history.

9. The Rest of the Story

All right...I'd made the decision. How was I going to make it happen?

Locate the remaining memorials, plan a route, find some support along the way, and come home; those were the broad strokes.

I sat, and I sat, and I sat at the computer, willing my fingers to work...a little voice telling me I was missing something important, and it wasn't coming. While my mind was saying "No sweat, just paint by the numbers from one to whatever, and the rest will take care of itself. This is doable," something deeper was trying to convince me that it really was going to be a big deal, and I was probably inadequate to the task.

And I was caught somewhere in between. I've learned since then that almost everyone who has ever done anything significant always had a doubt creep in till they got down to it, broke it down into pieces and proceeded to grind it out.

So, what did I need to do? I made a list. My list was an extremely fungible list. It grew and shrank...morphed from a "must have" list to an "If I can find it" document...eventually settling into a logical, if seemingly endless, number of tasks to perform in a limited amount of time. But it all worked out.

First things first: where are the memorials? How much research will be necessary? When do I stop? Push a button and pray?

Almost immediately I found a single website with more than 400 separate and specific Vietnam Veterans' memorials, and the ball started gathering momentum.

I set up a Facebook page for the Tour. My personal page took about three years to get to 1000 friends. I was hoping to have at least that many before the Tour began. As it turned out, Tour friends were very easy to find and within 6-8 months, or about half the time I was hoping to reach my first thousand, I had topped out at the 5000 maximum allowed by Facebook. This was a minor miracle in itself.

While I was expanding my research into the memorials, my FB friends all over the USA were sending me information on installations that I had not found and likely would not have known about but for their input. There were some dry holes to be sure...some that came my way were either inappropriate for my needs being entirely generic, temporary installations of the "Moving Walls" or just a result of incorrect information.

A generic memorial, in my interpretation, is one that honors all veterans from all campaigns without mentioning the campaigns, eras, or circumstances. My criteria for inclusion was it could be one memorial honoring veterans from several different campaigns on one stone or wall as long as it listed the campaigns separately. A distinction, I believe, with a difference.

In all, when I finally left home on May 31, 2013, I was looking forward to all I would see, all I would meet and all I would experience over the next calendar year.

* * * * *

The Fiscal Sponsor

I want to say emphatically that this could not have happened without the support, guidance and near constant assistance of the wonderful people at United Charitable Programs in Falls Church, Virginia.

I first learned about them from one of my friends at church who had used UCP to establish her own charitable foundation. Having heard over the years how difficult, expensive and intrusive it can be to go through the IRS to obtain a federally recognized non-profit status, I was intrigued enough to ask her how she did it.

Turns out, after less than a month and a few hundred dollars, she was ready to roll out her program. She put me in touch with the staff of UCP.

UCP is a Fiscal Sponsor; an enterprise set up for the express purpose of using their own non-profit status to approve and supervise smaller programs to operate more efficiently and within the law. While their policies and procedures are geared to be as non-intrusive as possible to the program directors, they are also designed to protect their own status, as they should.

From the first phone call I knew I was home. Their executive director Jan Ridgely turned out to be the perfect person to help me reach my objective. Smart, personable and passionate, she was intrigued by my idea and approved it in about a week. She was adept at guiding me through what I needed to know, steering me away from areas that could violate IRS guidelines, and recognizing when I was trying to "reinterpret" what she was saying to skate along that line that none shall cross. I know I must have been a trial to her in those early days but she never, ever, gave me anything but her best and most attentive self. And all those times I really wanted to hear a yes from her, rather than a constant refrain of "NO," turns out she was right each and every time, saving me from myself at every turn.

This relationship I forged with UCP is one of the very best I have ever been privileged to maintain. As you will read in later segments, their participation in my travels were crucial more than once.

Okay. Now I was official. This meant I could start asking people for money…contributions. How much fun was that going to be? As it turned out, not much.

Asking people for money has never been high on my list of things I like to do. But the financial resources came in, little by little, over time, so that on my first day of travel I had not nearly enough, but enough to get started with faith that the rest would come when and as needed.

The Web Site

While I can negotiate web sites, I can't create them myself. My mortgage company utilized a preplanned format that was just barely customizable enough to work for me. My friend Patti cobbled together a basic website for the bicycle company that worked well. But this was going to be the one that I needed to get right, a tool to show me for the person I was at the time, the person I had been in the service, back in the day, and convey all I was planning to do, and be compliant with UCP requirements.

I was referred to an angel named Maryann Brown who, over the phone, gave me an approximate price for building the site. She had immediate empathy for the project, as her father had also served in Vietnam. She was interested from the first minute we spoke. When I met with her for the first time and she was able to see the entire scope of the project, the context, and her own feelings about her father in particular and veterans in general, she offered to do it for free. I'm not that kind of guy. I paid her anyway. And this was before I had raised a dollar in contributions.

After listening to my half baked ideas and limited design abilities, Maryann really put herself into it and it evolved into something we were both proud of. That web site worked well for me for nearly three years and, while it is no longer up and running it was important at the time. For the first time I could see myself as I had been, and read about my life, what I had done with it and what I had become.

The crowning touch to the website was the itinerary; a way to connect the dots around the country that made sense. I built in an extra day here and there to give me some wiggle room with the schedule, and pinpointed where I'd be each and every day of the coming year. It was a six-week project just to produce the itinerary, and it was a true work of art.

So...now I had my legal stuff out of the way, a web site up and running, an itinerary, a *lot* of Facebook friends, and about six months to go before the projected start date of March 30, 2012. Then things took a turn.

10. *The Accident*

In September of 2011, while driving to meet some friends for some much needed R&R, I was waiting at an intersection for the light to change. This was at the height of rush hour in Denver on one of the slowest moving roads in town; one that seems to be terminally congested in the middle of the day, let alone during rush hour.

On this Friday evening, there was enough open space behind me that a distracted driver, weaving through sparse traffic, at a speed greater than conditions would permit, was able to hit me from behind hard enough to smash me into the car in front of me, lifting the rear of my car high enough that hers was almost totally buried under mine. When it came to rest, my rear wheels were embedded in her windshield, inches from her face.

Before the dust settled I was already a crazy person, seeing all this effort going down the drain and already anticipating the pain that would keep me in therapy for nearly a year. And knowing that my start date had just gone up in smoke.

I was right. I was rushed to the hospital, shaken but not quite broken, checked out, and was released after a few hours. I took a taxi home.

My poor car, crushed at both ends, was a total loss. And, as I mentioned, I was facing what turned out to be nearly a full year of physical therapy before I could even think about starting the Tour.

I was depressed beyond reason; not nearly to the point of hurting myself or becoming otherwise unmanageable, but bummed that more than a year of planning came to a furious halt. I put all my energies into a "poor me" state of mind and set aside further planning for most of that year.

Little by little life seemed to get worse. I didn't get out and do much, and I couldn't work like I was accustomed to. I was bored and restless most of the year and just a pain in the ass to be around.

Finally I was released from PT, turned to my attorney for some resolution, and waited. And waited.

Toward the end of the year, feeling somewhat better, I was able to pick up the reins of the project and continue planning. I could resume a full work schedule, which stopped the financial bleeding, and used my spare time building databases that I knew I would need along the way.

Sometime that year I had lunch with an amazing woman, Polly Letofsky, who several years before had walked around the world. *Around the freaking world.* It was a stroll that would take her five whole years and mold her into amazing condition while absorbing cultural traditions and influences most of us can only dream of experiencing. My venture seemed puny by comparison but I wanted her insight into my planning and preparation and to see if she had any suggestions. She gave me a lot of "you seem to be doing all the right things" and "don't worry, it'll all work out." And she was right. It was reassuring to know I had been doing many of the right things all along.

A true trailblazer, Polly's walk, on behalf of breast cancer awareness and cure was a huge success and raised hundreds of thousands of dollars. The walk is memorialized in her book 3 MPH, available on Amazon and other sources.

Eventually, the lawsuit from the crash was settled and the money was enough to get me back to square one financially with a little left over. I now had the time and the motivation to plan the *new* itinerary. This one would only take another month to redo.

11. Go Time

The hardest part of the new itinerary was picking the new start date of May 31, 2013, and making the new dates flow intelligently. Matching places and dates with weather patterns and other criteria was just as challenging as the first go-round.

I had my completed databases...more than 3000 of my FB friends listed alphabetically as well as by state. I had the American Legion, the VFW and the VVA posts identified in each and every city in which I planned to stop. I made a list of all the churches affiliated with my home church along the way. I identified people I knew in various places around the country: family and friends, and sometimes friends of friends who might give me shelter and support.

I began an inventory of what I would need to take along to support myself for a full year on the road. It was an impressive list. It included:

Safety and survival gear

Camping stuff in case I needed to pitch a camp or sleep in the car

Two suitcases…one for pants & shirts and one for socks
& skivvies
Toiletries and sundry items
Tech stuff in case it was needed
Non-perishable food items, just in case
A whole box of books
Copies of my entire CD collection, in two big binders
The traveling photo suite I had purchased
Five cameras
Two computers
A 10" tablet with two GPS apps, just in case
My guitar
And all the paperwork I needed along the way.

After the accident I had purchased a Ford Freestyle, my first station wagon…ever; shorter and wider than an Explorer, and more aerodynamic, which helped manage fuel costs along the way. Everything fit just enough to give good rear visibility for safety, and ease of access from the rear or either side door.

Additionally, if the need ever came up and I was stuck for shelter, the back laid out nearly seven feet in length. This was perfect for all 6' of me to lay down comfortably, and while I packed for the purpose, it didn't happen till the next to last night of the trip when, just for the hell of It, I pulled into a campsite in Cape Girardeau, MO and used all that stuff I had been carting around for nearly a year.

A local sign and banner company owned by a retired AF officer was able to create mini wraps for both sides and the rear windshield, logos large enough that people would be able to see me coming from a long way away. I was nearly ready.

* * * * *

So here it was, the jumping-off day. Armed with about $3,500 in cash and a little over $4,000 in donations, a lot of faith in front of me and prayer behind me, I set off for a year on the road.

12. May 31, 2013

Somewhere along the way, during the run-up to getting on the road, I got the feeling there would be some fanfare; not THAT much, you understand. Maybe some music, speeches from a few dignitaries, an early morning party with friends and a motorcycle escort for the first hundred miles or so.

The reality was I got up in the morning to an empty house, got myself together, said one final prayer for the success of the journey and the good I intended to do along the way, walked out to my pre-packed car and headed east not long after the sun started to rise on its way to meeting me somewhere halfway.

Those last few days were a little tense. Only four days before, a deadly tornado ripped through Moore, Oklahoma heralding the start of tornado season. I would enter Oklahoma on the fourth day of the Tour, according to my itinerary. People were telling me not to go, to wait a while, let the weather play itself out.

By this time I had already set my support schedule for the first several weeks and people were expecting me. No way was

I going to go back to the drawing board and chart out another itinerary, call back all the people who had offered up their hospitality and reschedule on account of a few potentially windy days.

So I headed first to Wyoming, Nebraska, Kansas and Oklahoma before skirting a corner of Arkansas, a bit more of Kansas, winding up the first week and about 1300 miles in Kansas City. Piece of cake. But I got off to a very unsettling start.

Once on the road I put in a call to the Legion contact that had promised me a room in Kearney, Nebraska only to find out he was out of town and had forgotten I was coming. I was pissed but managed to keep it together.

So with eyes rolling so far back into my head that I could almost see myself thinking, we talked out a solution and, from a distance, he was able to set it up with his post to greet me warmly and well.

It was a great place to start the journey. Upon arrival at the post I was greeted enthusiastically and invited to visit the local memorial with two of the members of VFW Post 759.

As memorials go it was…modest: a piece of deteriorating bronze atop a waist-high block of marble and a flagpole. I knew I wasn't going to see something grand and huge and magnificent at each site but I was really hoping for more. However, it was sacred to them. That fact was illustrated to me in the next moment when one of my companions began "policing" the area, picking up some trash and pulling a couple of weeds around the installation.

I asked, "Are you the official caretakers of the memorial site?" One responded, "No, we just do it. We asked the city if we could be the memorial's official caretakers and they said, 'sure, but you have to take care of the whole park.' "

"End of discussion," the other said, "so we just do it."

The bronze plate was corroded and pitted, but age and weather will do that to metal. It was by no means the worst I would see around the nation in terms of wear, and the area was lovingly maintained by a very devoted band of local brothers in arms.

After a night in a local motel I was off to a city I had traveled through many times but never stopped to explore: Junction City, KS.

My host for the day/night, Anthony Gibson, Commander of the local VFW post, was extremely gracious. It was a post of predominantly black veterans and the post itself was a virtual museum to the memory of the Buffalo Soldiers. The photos, plaques and other memorabilia were a slice of life I had heard about over the years but never witnessed this intimately. The members were buzzing around the post getting ready for an annual activity they participate in, feeding the cast and crew of the Soldier's Show at Kansas State University in Manhattan that night. This is a musical revue featuring talented soldiers from all over the Army that tours the world performing for military and civilian audiences alike. They were very, very good.

African American soldiers have been a part of every major American war. The Buffalo Soldiers, officially the 10th Infantry out of Fort Leavenworth, Kansas, was formed in 1866, one of six all black army units, all of which operated west of the Mississippi. While the source of the name "Buffalo Soldiers" remains an official mystery, the prevailing theory is that it was due to the thick coats made from buffalo hide that protected them during harsh winters. The term was used respectfully and with honor, a tradition carried on by the current members of VFW Post 6406, Junction City, KS.

I joined the Post in taking care of those that currently take care of us. It was fulfilling to me to take care of some very special active duty soldiers, and they appreciated it. I also found a memorial on the campus I had not expected, the first of many I would discover along the way.

We finished, cleaned up, returned to Post, and I could finally get to my hotel room and relax after a very long and rewarding day.

* * * * *

Passing through Wichita to Winfield, Kansas was definitely taking a path less traveled. While I am pretty familiar with the trip across Kansas from Denver to Kansas City, this was the first time I had crossed the state from top to bottom. Saw a LOT of corn, a sight that became one of my more or less constant companions for months.

In Winfield I was warmly welcomed into the local post where I met, among others, Stephen Markley, a Vietnam vet and former radio personality, now retired in this small Kansas town. With two of his buddies we attempted to record an interview in the post but were stymied by the background noises… the clinking of glasses and snapping of Zippo lighters was too much to deal with.

We decided to go to the local memorial, only a couple blocks from the post, to do the interview. The setting was perfect…a gorgeous June day, the memorial an elegant backdrop for three colorful vets and their stories. The memorial itself was a mini-wall, patterned after The Wall in Washington DC, with the names of the Kansas casualties from Vietnam. Also set in a slight hollow in the center of a park, it was the ideal place for the interview.

About half an hour later we disbanded and I went, finally, to my hotel room and uploaded the interview only to discover a problem with the sound. I had a beautiful if silent video and no time for a do-over. I did return to Winfield on the way home at the end of the Tour in hopes of redoing the interview but Stephen was the only one I could find, and there was just no way. One opportunity lost. One big lesson learned: double and triple check the sound quality before the interview.

On to Oklahoma. Only about ten days before, severe tornados tore through outlying areas of Oklahoma City, creating a devastating and dramatic start to their annual tornado season. But rescheduling this soon was just not an option. I headed for Tulsa and a meeting with Ray Hildreth, a Vietnam vet and author of a moving and thrilling first-person adventure entitled *Hill 488*.

Hill 488, the story of his company's patrol, staking out a hilltop to observe and report, turned into a major battle that resulted in the deaths of nearly half of the squad and multiple wounds for every defender who survived. It was riveting and hard to put down. I read through it quickly.

Ray now operates a martial arts school in Tulsa, making use of his skills as a warrior, teaching firsthand the concepts of respect and discipline, self preservation and initiative; the same skills that allowed him and the others in his combat team to survive so many years ago. It was a privilege to spend time with him in conversation and watch him work with his students.

The next day found me in Henryetta, Oklahoma, about eighty miles or so due east of Oklahoma City, and the hometown of NFL star Troy Aikman. My host for the stay was a terrific man, Mike Doak, another Vietnam vet. Mike worked harder on behalf of local veterans and other civic causes than any man I have ever met. I honestly have no idea how he found time to make a living.

Mike set up three events for me during my one day in Henryetta: a luncheon speaking engagement about three minutes after I arrived in the city, a small gathering at the local library for another brief talk, and a pancake breakfast the next morning.

Mike is a born and bred Henryettan and has a clear recollection of the town in the '60's. He and other local boys served in and survived Vietnam and came back to resume their lives. One man did not. The town of Henryetta during that time was overwhelmingly white. Mike told me there were only three African-American families living in Henryetta at the time. Most of the local black families lived in the nearby city of Clearview, one of a handful of cities in Oklahoma created for and settled entirely by African-Americans. Henryetta's sole fatality from southeast Asia was the son of one of the black families.

Turns out that deceased veteran, Anthony Warren Grundy, Lance Corporal, United States marine Corps, twenty years of age, was ultimately denied burial in the Henryetta cemetery. Hearing this story I was instantly ashamed. This young man who gave up everything to serve his country was seriously disrespected by his city.

I remember the '60's pretty well. I remember the struggles in the south over historical practices of segregation, and the birth of the civil rights movement. I especially remember the Watts riots in South Central L.A. in 1965, my first year in uniform.

Watts, Detroit and other violent domestic incidents were in cities involving American citizens, not an enemy half a world away. I had not stopped to consider Oklahoma as part of that struggle. I hardly considered Oklahoma at all for that matter. I had never been there and, outside of the musical that was produced when I was very young, the place was largely irrelevant to me. It is now clearer than ever to me that racism was not a southern thing, or a major metropolitan thing, but a national thing, and continues to rear its ugly head in ways subtle and not so subtle around the country.

Over the years racial tensions in the Henryetta/Clearview area have largely vanished and veterans from both cities get together regularly to care for the Clearview cemetery. Their brotherhood was evident that morning at the pancake breakfast in Clearview, following a tour of the cemetery. The small local church/meeting hall opened up and about a dozen of us, black and white, spent a warm couple of hours meeting, sharing stories and taking measure of each other. It was a special time, and I am grateful to Mike for caring enough to set it all up. Without that early support and the donations received during that visit, mine would have been a very different journey. And, Mike, wherever you are and whatever you are doing, I know it is more for us than it is for yourself.

* * * * *

Rogers, Arkansas is the home of Bill Freeman and Barbara Aguirre, and one of the most active American Legion posts I visited on the entire journey. I had no idea what they were doing on behalf of local homeless veterans till I arrived. All I had done was call ahead looking for some local support, a place to sleep, someone to interview—possibly a donation, without realizing what an important contribution they were already making in the area.

Keep in mind that one of my goals on this journey was to find veterans who were giving back to other veterans in ways large and small. While my focus was on Vietnam veterans, it was no matter to me which campaign they represented or served.

"Operation Reboot" was an accident waiting to happen, a fortuitous accident; one of those things that begins as a chore and ends up a calling.

One day, as the story goes, Barbara, the Post Commander, got a call: "We have a vet who needs a pot to cook with. He's been off the street for a couple months and has been cooking in a borrowed pot and eating off paper plates because he has nothing. The owner wants his pot back. Can you help? This man had been in an apartment for two months with nothing: no bed or bedding, no furniture, basically four empty walls."

"Our post hosts bingo," Barbara said, "and one night I told the ladies about this veteran and asked if they had anything they could spare. A few days later I arrived at the post and couldn't get in because of all the donations. I rented a storage unit and it quickly filled up. I rented another and it filled up as well."

Given the mission, Barbara and her post buddies Art and Cliff started working the phone, with a lot of pushing and pulling, groveling and negotiating.

And the donations kept coming in. By the time I arrived in Rogers, sixteen months had passed since that first veteran had been assisted. In the intervening year plus, they had replicated that service to sixty-eight veterans taken off the street, and given hope and a little dignity, and, in the interim, managed to stockpile enough furnishings, etc. to fill a warehouse and two rental storage units.

"How it works," according to Barbara, "is we give them a 'bucket' that has four plates, four cups, four place settings of utensils. They don't care if the plates are blue or red or green, as long as they don't have to eat off paper."

I was able to tour their warehouse and meet their "staff" of eleven, mostly retired veterans assisted ably by a couple of very young "recruits." I filmed them working, arranging, loading, sorting, folding and doing the 101 tasks an operation of this magnitude generates. At that time they received no funding from any official source, including the national headquarters of the Legion, they just plow on using their existing resources as responsibly as possible.

Barbara continued, "It's not just the newer vets coming back. People have scars from different wars and we as a nation have to be able to react to that, and not just when you see a homeless veteran—'oh that's so sad'—of course it's sad, but you get up off your butt and do something about it."

It has been more than a year since my visit but I know that if I went back today I would still find them hard at work on behalf of their brother and sister veterans: a truly inspiring group of incredible heart.

Barbara knew of another post in the southern part of the state that had a similar program going. She took her idea to the Legion's state convention and presented it to the gathering. She believed the program will spread to the rest of the state over time.

Word of these activities eventually leaks into the consciousness of the public, but I hope they have some way of letting the entire American Legion world know about what they have done and that each and every post in America gets on board.

Thank you Barbara, Bill, Cliff, Art and all the rest of you generous souls.

Note: As of August, 2014, according to their Facebook Page, the Legion post in Rogers, AR has furnished a total of 148 apartments for previously homeless veterans.

In addition there is news that Art Abbott, one of those who graciously gave of his time while I was visiting, recently passed. As their procurement officer he was an important piece of their operation and will be missed.

13. June 7, 2013

It is a short hop from Rogers, Arkansas to Branson, Missouri, but a giant leap culturally. Branson is well known to people as an entertainment destination that fills the valley in which it is located. There are dozens of theaters, concert halls, comedy clubs, tourist traps, etc. scattered throughout downtown Branson. The most outrageous example was the Titanic Theater: a full scale reproduction of the ship (from bow to amidships) fronting a large theater to port. It sits in a manmade "ocean" with fountains at the waterline spraying back a simulated "wake." The building was almost worth the trip all by itself.

Catty-corner to the ship is a diner, Jackie B. Goode's, and the principal reason for my visit. The owner of the diner, David L. Goode, lost his older brother in Vietnam. Upon purchasing the restaurant, he named it after the brother, Jack, a true hero. While wounded in action, Jack continued to hold back the enemy, saving his buddies at the cost of his own life. He was posthumously awarded the Purple Heart along with a Bronze Star *and* a Silver Star. On a wall in the foyer of the restaurant stands a tribute in honor of the fallen soldier, proudly displayed by his brother. An honor, indeed.

A modest drive to the state capitol the following day brought me to two interesting memorial sites, the first in Springfield National Cemetery. This cemetery is truly a national treasure, completely filled with the remains of citizens from our entire history, including the recently re- interred widow of a Revolutionary War officer. Her remains, at the family's request, were relocated from further east. This was more living history than I ever knew in Colorado or growing up in California.

The Missouri Veterans' Cemetery, my next stop also in Springfield, is home to a number of large memorials, representing several conflicts, spread over many, many acres. As I made my way slowly through the grounds, snapping photos of statues, steles, markers and stones of all kinds, I eventually found the section that hosted the Vietnam Veterans' memorial. It sits adjacent to a chapel in the center of a wide expanse of green.

When I arrived, a funeral service for a recently deceased Vietnam veteran was being conducted. I sat for a while taking in the space, the serenity, the sense of pride and caring of the community, and I prayed.

When the ceremony concluded, and the friends and family filed outside, I felt a need to go to them and pay my respects to the fallen brother. Many of them were veterans and I was made to feel welcomed into their community. It was a singular experience on my journey.

Moving on, I crossed back into Kansas for a visit to the University of Pittsburg which hosted a memorial on campus. I was unprepared for what I saw. This was the grandest memorial of the journey to date. Like The Wall in D.C. which is all but invisible before you are right on it, this amphitheater-like installation sits in a natural bowl and you are forced to walk up several steps before you are able to look down into it.

In addition to the usual brass plaques and bronzes is a reflecting pond surrounded by bricks etched with the names of the fallen. Behind the pool is a large pylon with an homage to the veterans, and behind it stood a half-sized replica of The Wall in D.C. complete with all 58,000+ names, and behind that, a display of flags of all 50 states blowing in the Kansas wind.

Because of its size and the unique bowl in which it sits, it was impossible to capture the entire memorial in a single frame. But I tried.

There were also several notable quotations etched into the polished marble of the memorial including:

"Honor to the soldier and sailor everywhere who bravely bears his country's cause."—*Abraham Lincoln*

"God grants liberty only to those who live it, and are always ready to defend it."—*Daniel Webster*

"From this day to the ending of the world…we in it shall be remembered…we band of brothers: for he today that sheds his blood with me shall be my brother."
—*William Shakespeare, from Henry V*

I had no idea the root of the expression "Band of Brothers" hailed from so far back, guess I was reading other things in high school, but as we will see in East Meadow on Long Island, later in this story, the expression fits all military men and women from all conflicts.

* * * * *

Sunday, June 9th, I was expecting the unexpected on my arrival in KC. I had arranged a speaking engagement at the Center for Spiritual Living Church (CSL) in Kansas City, but had not secured any lodging or other support. There was family from my stepfather's side in nearby Missouri, but they were unable to host. I turned to another option on the Kansas side and it was an awkward and anxious five minutes.

My father passed away in Kansas City in 1998, surrounded by his family at the time. I was in Denver celebrating my own birthday when I got word of his passing. I was aware of his ongoing physical challenge and had recently visited him in the hospital in Shawnee Mission, Kansas, and his determination to get well, get back home and continue living his life, but it wasn't to be.

At the time, he was married to Thelma, a very nice Filipino woman, a nurse, and enjoyed a great relationship with her extended family, mostly other medical professionals. My sister and I had several interactions with Thelma's family and we liked them, but we were never got as close as we might have been. After the funeral we never saw them and rarely spoke on the phone. No reason for it, really, just the way life happened.

I found the home of Thelma's sister Aricely and knocked on the door. She came to the door, recognized me right away, and it was as though I had never been away; like I had gone to the store for some milk or a loaf of bread and had been away only minutes.

I never got to see Thelma during my brief stay, although we did talk for a while on the phone. She was preparing to retire and go back to the Philippines. I suspect the whole family is back there by now. I wound up spending several nights at the home of their stepson Larry and was at once grateful for their collective generosity and a little guilty that I had let seventeen years go by without as much as a hello. Rekindling old relationships was to be a recurrent theme on the Tour. It made me realize just how isolated and small I had let my life become in ways I had not thought possible.

During that time I was able to use Larry's home as a hub to visit outlying memorials in several Kansas cities, including two each in Topeka and Lawrence, and individual markers in Emporia, Lyndon, St. Mary's and Merriam. Small town America is full of reminders of the sacrifices of its sons and daughters.

The Center for Spiritual Living, Kansas City, led by Rev. Dr. Chris Michaels, welcomed me warmly and graciously and gave me time during the service to speak to those attending, tell my story and receive a few donations. Thank you, Rev. Chris.

Around the corner and down the street from the Church sits the Kansas City Vietnam Veterans' Memorial. I had first seen it during a trip to the city when my father was in the hospital, perhaps two months before his passing. I was surprised and pleased with its size, scope and location, ranking right up there with the others I had visited in DC and Kentucky. It was a full city block of walls, fountains, pools, walkways and reminders in the heart of the city.

I spent a good hour or so visiting on this beautiful June day, remembering, tearing up a time or two, offering a heartfelt prayer, shooting as many photos as I could and just knowing that I was on the right path. After several days there, it was time to move on.

14. June 13, 2013

Before journeying to California to live among prospectors and other denizens of early California, Mark Twain, born Samuel Langhorne Clemens, made his mark, pun intended, on and along the Wide Mississippi. His stories of Tom, Huck and Becky live on in schools and the hearts of children as great American literature, and deservedly so. I was excited at the prospect of visiting the area around Hannibal, Missouri, Twain's legendary hometown and was not disappointed.

Deep in the Ozarks lays Mark Twain Lake, a huge reservoir that twisted and turned, fingers stretching to the highway and back, among some of the most heart-stoppingly beautiful scenery imaginable. Massive bridges, and boats of all sizes and shapes passing under and around. And in one place near the Clarence Cannon Dam, sits a beautiful memorial to those citizens of the area lost in Vietnam.

Made of a composite material resembling granite, the gnomon, or pointer, of a sundial emerged from ground level and cast its shadow over a group of twelve composite "stones" set in an arc, with bronze faces marking the twelve months of the year. Each stone is engraved with the names of their lost boys according to the month in which they were KIA.

Flags flew high behind the stone markers and a soldier's cross stood at the foot of the gnomon. And from the cross, looking lakeward, is a marvelous expanse of water and forest forming a vista of peace and serenity to honor the fallen for all time; a blessing for the community.

The next day I visited Hannibal proper and was greeted by images and reminders of Mark Twain everywhere I turned; signs on buildings, street names, stores and restaurants, all continuing the theme of honoring the city's greatest son. And, in a park in the middle of town, is a small bronze plaque in honor of its veterans. After visiting the memorial I couldn't resist moseying down to the water's edge, taking off my shoes and socks, and wading into the "Big Muddy" for the first time.

I had located Wayne Zumwalt, one of my old shipmates, who still lived in the area where he grew up. I managed to get him on the phone but, as a farmer with thirty acres to harvest on the day I was passing through, there was no time to visit with him. My host for the visit, Bill Wright, also knew Wayne. He drove me by Wayne's farm, and I could see that he had indeed prospered over the forty-plus years since we left the service. Well into his 60's, he was still hard at work each day.

A couple days later I wound up in Wentzville, not far from St. Louis. I looked up the memorial that had been, for several years, a touchstone, widely thought to be the very first memorial to the veterans of the Vietnam War. This memorial, way ahead of its time, is a simple marble column with an eagle at the top and a bronze marker at the foot. It was dedicated in December of 1967, shortly after my ship arrived in Vietnam, and several months before we began our cruise back to "the World."

A little way down the road, St Louis beckoned.

* * * * *

Through the aid of the CSL center in St Louis and its wonderful Senior Minister, Marigene de Rusha, I was welcomed into the home of one of its members, Debbie Koebel, as a guest for several nights and given an opportunity to speak at the church that Sunday. Rev. Marigene is an enthusiastic and passionate leader and had her flock thoroughly entertained by the time I got up to speak, and just went with the flow. I enjoyed myself immensely and left with the service ringing in my ears the rest of the day.

After nearly three weeks without a break I was ready for some R&R. Debbie took me on a tour of the city that I'll bet few people get. We feasted on a signature St. Louis-style pizza, and gorged on gooey butter cake, another St. Louis original. We did the obligatory visit to the top of the Gateway Arch and even had time for a Cardinals baseball game. It was good to see Matt Holiday, one of my favorite former Colorado Rockies players, in action again. And he had a great night at the plate.

Near the Arch, in the heart of the city, is their Court of Honor, on a park-like island that runs several blocks along the center of Market St. Among the many memorials to past conflicts sits a large Vietnam Veterans' memorial made up of several distinct elements stretching for most of a city block. It is definitely an island of peace and reflection in the center of a vital and bustling metropolitan area.

Cape Girardeau was my next destination. I had a pleasant drive along the Mississippi, en route to one of the more picturesque cities I had seen so far. I was welcomed at the local VFW Post 38 by its Commander, Bill Humphrey, and manager, Pete. I was even treated to a stay at a nice local motel. Once they fed and watered me and sent me on my way, I was able to get a good rest to set me up for the next day's leg. Many thanks to both gentlemen are in order. The next day I crossed the Mississippi for the first time into Indiana and Kentucky.

Crossing the river into Illinois was, well, interesting. Gasoline in Illinois is/was the most expensive in the nation, even higher than in California. But the views in that little tri-state area were well worth the visit: the rolling hills, winding rivers, corn everywhere, century-old buildings and farms, through Mounds and finally Metropolis, home of—you guessed it—Superman. The pride of Metropolis is a twenty-foot tall statue to the Man of Steel, and most of the touristy stuff in the city revolves around this relationship with the fictional hero.

The Vietnam Veterans memorial in Metropolis, simple and elegant, was one of the most moving of the entire Tour, thanks to a few incredible words inscribed near the bottom, words that I worked into my prayer at each memorial to come:

> To the Fallen—Honor
> To the Captive—Freedom
> To the Returned—Solace
> To the Wounded—Healing
> To the Missing—Repatriation
> To the Future—Peace

I carry them with me always.

I dipped a little south across the Ohio River into Paducah, Kentucky, to see their memorial. Paducah was special in my mind; a city involved in the storyline of the movie *In Country*. I wish I could have had a longer visit.

Something remarkable did happen, however. I received a call from Tamara Heater, a kindred spirit if ever there was one. I had somehow entered her consciousness in passing through the St Louis area at the same time as a Traveling Wall. She thanked me for being part of the Traveling Wall before I could tell her that I was not part of that effort. It was a common misconception throughout the Tour.

Traveling Walls have been circulating around the country for several years. Typically, a Traveling Wall is a 50-80% scale reproduction of The Wall in Washington DC set up in conjunction with holidays, especially those important to veterans, and remain for several days. Other exhibits generally accompany the Traveling Walls providing the public with additional information about our time in Vietnam and they provide local residents who may never get to DC an opportunity to witness the memorial.

We had a nice conversation and became fast friends. She actually drove down to Paducah to meet with me. Turned out she was an internet whiz who had some ideas about increasing my effectiveness on the internet, and before I knew it, I had a new website that was visually stunning and interactive, a quality lacking in my previous website.

In coming up with a name for the Tour, it seemed perfectly logical and clear to me what the Vietnam Veterans' Memorial Tour was and was meant to be. However, soon after beginning my travels, I got used to people assuming I had something to do with the Traveling Walls. Not exactly. I have seen one or another of the Traveling Walls in several cities around the country, and I value the work that those involved with the Traveling Walls actually do, more than I can adequately say here. The physical work, transporting, setting up and breaking down the panels every few days; the emotional toll of reading the list of names of the fallen, answering

> questions, dealing with people of multiple genera-
> tions and experience, and assisting those who are
> deeply affected by the installation's power and
> magnitude. They are well and truly some of the
> most dedicated and passionate veterans it has
> been my good fortune to know. You are all blessed.

Back in the car, back across the Ohio River and north for a few days through central Illinois. Corn everywhere I looked. I enjoyed taking back roads through country that I had never seen before, taking it slow and easy, trying to keep a low profile and conserve fuel. The itinerary had been planned so that I would have a relatively easy drive each and every day, except for the southwest and its challenging distances between cities. So far it was working.

I weaved my way through Flora, Centralia, Vandalia and Mulberry Grove, through Springfield and ended up in Mt. Pulaski, at the home of Bob McCue of American legion post 447. Bob is an elderly veteran, a product of the Korean War, but he made me feel at home from the first minute. We had some exceptionally crisp chicken for dinner, courtesy of his granddaughter, and spent the evening chit-chatting and watching TV; an experience I had not had in nearly two months.

Back to Springfield. The Oakridge Cemetery in the heart of the city has truly wonderful memorials to the Illinois veterans of all the major conflicts of the 20th century. The most visible and contemporary of them is the Vietnam Veterans' memorial, a structure that honors all the fallen from each service branch in its own wing. Thank you, Springfield.

15. June 22, 2013

I had been looking forward to the next night since before the journey began. The plan included locating friends all across the country and enlisting them for some local support. My friends (and my sister's BFF) Kay and Don Norton had relocated from Southern California to Macomb, Illinois, long before I moved to Denver, and have made a wonderful home for themselves. Not only were they the most gracious hosts imaginable, but we toured their city and even found a Vietnam Veterans' Memorial in the heart of their city that had escaped my radar. We spent some time at the memorial then went for ice cream.

I had seen Kay earlier that year when she came to Denver to see her son Donnie, a gifted musician, perform near Greeley, Colorado. He was a music major at the University of Northern Colorado. I hadn't seen Don since they left California. Again, it was like no time at all had passed. It was that natural and good.

Havana, Carthage and Rock Island were next on my list. I could see Iowa from where I was, although I wouldn't get there till later in the year. A side trip took me to Wiota, Wisconsin and back south to Rockford (Home of the Rockford Peaches of the Women's All-American Baseball League, featured in the terrific movie *A League of Their Own.*), east to Waukegan and a wandering route through some of the northern suburbs and, finally, into the heart of Chicago.

* * * * *

Gotta say, Chicago is a cleaner town than I remembered, but also a meaner town. Parking is ferociously expensive in the city. Gas was $4.55 a gallon in June of 2013, and the parking meters played tricks on the psyche; a perfect example of the principle "more is less."For example, in Denver (as in most of the country), if you put a quarter in the parking meter you get, let's say, fifteen minutes. Another quarter pays for fifteen more minutes, and so on.

In Chicago, not so much. The first quarter gets you fifteen minutes, but the second quarter only nets you twelve minutes more. A third quarter is worth 10 more minutes, and so on. I had heard about the high taxes and political shenanigans in Chicago over the years but this was the first time I had witnessed it firsthand.

Now, I *did* spend a lot of time in Chicago during the summer of '65 when I was in my Class A technical school at the great Lakes Naval Training Center, just to the north. But our weekends were a little different back then. We had just enough money for train fare into the city, a few drinks and a cheap dinner, then back to base; sometimes so broke we had to give blood downtown to have enough money to party with. And, of course, it doesn't take as much alcohol to get drunk after giving blood, which worked out just fine for us. If memory serves, our pay as E-2s(one stripe above a recruit) was about $18.00 a week.

There were several memorials in and around Chicago, including one man's version of an in country "Hootch," a semi-temporary improvised hut, sometimes partially underground and reinforced against enemy fire. It sits out in his front yard.

The principal Chicago memorial is set in Wabash Plaza, down a flight of steps to the walkway near the Chicago River. Stairs on either side guide you down to the plaza where a commemorative wall of names is installed on the retaining wall, fronting a reflecting pool and fountain. On one side is a series of levels with concrete benches and brilliant green swaths of grass ascending to the street, allowing people to sit, meditate, read, have lunch, and socialize in this magnificent setting.

In addition, Chicago is home to the National Vietnam Veterans' Art Museum, a product of the collective mind of a group of vets who assembled and curated an incredible array of art created entirely by Vietnam veterans. There are photographs, paintings, sculptures and other installations, all evocative of the psyche of the war. All together, the collection contains some 2500 pieces, in a rotating display.

Joe Fornelli was the museum's front man during my visit. One of the original members of the Vietnam Veterans' Art Group that eventually became the museum, Joe is a veteran of the war himself, Army, 1965, door gunner on a UH-1D, better known as a Huey. Thank you, Joe, for your service then and your continued service now.

One exhibit I wanted badly to see was their well-known ceiling display of hanging dog tags…a large array of more than 58,000 tags on chains. It had been the centerpiece of their former location. Forced to move a while back, their current space is not large enough to allow its display. The entire piece is held in storage for another day.

Four days in Chicago went by very quickly, sightseeing, sampling local foods, especially Chicago-style pizza, and enjoying the company of a gracious and generous CSL minister, Rev. Celeste Frazier. She was kind enough to open her home to me for four nights on very short notice.

My last stop in Illinois was just at the south edge of the Chicago Metro area, Lansing. Close to my destination it became clear the memorial was set at the edge of a large commercial/industrial area adjacent to the Lansing airport. From a couple blocks away I could see the Huey hovering over the corner. I pulled into the complex, looking around for all the activity I would have expected. It was deserted. I headed directly to the memorial.

It was obvious that a lot of thought and effort went into the design and execution of this space. There was the large, segmented, smooth black granite wall fronting the pylon upon which sat the retired Huey. The wall was full of words, names, dates and images. There were stone markers leading the way...a cobbled walkway and viewing area, bare flagpoles, and weeds... lots of weeds. Piles of leaves blown around by the wind sat in tufts here and there.

It was also clear that the site had been abandoned quite some time ago, and equally clear that some veterans do show up from time to time to take care of the memorial as best they can. But time and nature will intrude on the best of intentions. It is a magnificent memorial, designed to greet crowds and host events, and I was the only one there that day.

Through research and by scanning thousands of photos of memorials designed and installed over several decades, my assumption was that many would be in some state of disrepair. Over the course of the Tour I was proved both right and wrong. While some were set up in obscure and seemingly forgotten locations, and others were in prominent places but clearly showing their age, there was only a handful that were actually broken, battered and otherwise left to decay. In fact, I found several examples of groups and individuals whose mission in life is the proper care and maintenance of their memorial site, even if it needs to be carried out under the local radar.

16. *July 1, 2013*

It was a casual, unhurried trip through Indiana for the first few days. All the memorials from Rockville through Princeton were interesting, mostly similar and all on the grounds of their respective County Courthouses. I learned in that part of the country, in fact, over the year in many parts of the country, that courthouse lawns double as memorial gardens to all of our major campaigns, many all the way back to the Civil war and, in others, the Revolutionary War. I was, figuratively, tripping through our entire history on my quest.

And there were the unexpected moments when just random things would catch my eye apropos to absolutely nothing at the time, like the billboard I flew past advertising "Amish-Style Cooking at the Schwartz Family Restaurant" in Eckerty, Indiana, a town so small it wasn't even on my map. Wonder what Amish-style gefilte fish tastes like? But I digress.

Evansville was a welcome stop. It is a beautiful, if antique, city with a still bustling port. Jerry Blake, an active member of his local Legion post, was my host for the visit and snagged me a room at the local hotel/casino complex. How could I gracefully refuse? I love to gamble, especially on blackjack, and usually win slightly more often than I lose. But on the Tour I was certainly blessed at the tables, and casinos along my entire route contributed more than they know to my cause.

Jerry got me situated and left me to my own devices. It was raining pretty steadily that evening so I didn't get out, but the next morning during a break in the drizzle I managed to take a walk down by the banks of the Ohio River. I shot some photos of the memorial that sat just off the walking path, and just to the east of the Four Freedoms Memorial, four Greek inspired columns representing our basic rights as Americans, surrounded by stone markers representing all fifty states.

A few blocks away, a little west and away from the river, was a second, smaller memorial to the war. After visiting both I started back to the hotel as the rain once again fell. I packed up, checked out and got back on the road.

Crossing the river into Kentucky once again, I drove to Henderson. Less corn, more greenery and varied landscapes awaited me. In case I haven't mentioned it enough, corn was pretty much a constant roadside attraction for more than a month and would continue to show up in virtually every state I visited.

An added benefit to finally being out of Illinois: Gasoline just across the border in Kentucky dropped by a full third, and in Indiana, even less.

The memorial in Henderson was beautifully situated in a local park. The rain was still falling, and in my photographs it appears as though the stone markers are weeping. It was an emotional jolt.

Finishing southern Indiana, I wound up in Lawrenceburg, close onto the border with Ohio. This made the early ballot for one of my favorite cities in the USA: picturesque and uncrowded, historical yet modern where it needs to be, with a memorial walk near the river, and a port area that harkens back to the days of Tom Sawyer and Huck Finn. It was home to two unforgettable memorials: the first a substantial memorial to the local heroes of Vietnam near the courthouse, and, by the waterfront, a beautiful multi-figure statue in honor of first responders of all types.

That night found me in Cincinnati, in the home of some pretty wonderful people.

17. *July 3, 2013*

To my knowledge, Cincinnati is the largest city in the country that has no Vietnam-era memorial. But it does have an active and vital CSL center. Thanks to the gracious and accessible Rev. Linda Ketchum, a bed was found for me in the home of members of the center.

Robert and Theresa Slusher opened their home in Newport, Kentucky to me, and treated me to a wonderful evening. Newport is just across the river from Cincinnati proper, so close to the baseball stadium that you can imagine a home run landing in their yard. We left their home and walked a couple blocks to the river and over the bridge, a refreshing change from driving, had dinner and went to a movie; almost too normal a night for words, considering how the previous month had gone.

My support system in Dayton had broken down. The local CSL center, despite their best effort, was unable to find me a sponsor for the visit. I do want to thank Legion Commanders John Paynter of Middletown and Pete Regules of Zanesville for stepping up on my behalf. Their support at that moment was important. The three days I spent in their part of Ohio took me to several interesting memorials:

Mt. Carmel: A local park with memorials to a single soldier, all local veterans who did not return, the air cavalry (Huey up on blocks), women who served in Vietnam, Gold Star Mothers and war dogs.

Middleton: A whole plaza complete with a beautifully etched graphic wall, the names of local heroes, individual bricks on the plaza floor and more.

Dayton: A memorial ring in their Vietnam Veterans' Memorial park with multiple individual markers.

Fairborn: Home to the USAF National Museum complex, with a memorial garden the size of several football fields, and markers honoring all conflicts with aviation components, individual actions and units, and especially the Forward Air Controllers of Vietnam.

Groveport: Home to a smaller-scale museum devoted strictly to Vietnam, complete with riverine craft, multiple helos, artillery and ground assault craft and many memorial markers on the grounds, as well as an indoor display of many smaller, more personal items. Many thanks to docent Barbara Barber for a thorough tour.

Ohio is cemented in my mind as the state to have the most large-scale installations, specific to our time in Vietnam, than any other state in the country. I felt blessed to be able to visit and take in each and every one of them, and I appreciate the time, effort, money and psychic debt that each represents. Thank you, Ohio. Next up, West Virginia.

* * * * *

In little more than a month this journey stripped away many of my preconceptions about most of this country. Like most of my generation I have done my share of traveling around the country, but always in a kind of bubble, or state of mind that made me uncritical of my surroundings.

Did I notice accents? Sure. Gross differences from area to area? Absolutely! But not enough to get a real sense of where I was and what I was experiencing. On this trip I was determined to stay aware, and, boy, was I.

I noticed that Kansas could be green and golden, not the muted brown that I was used to seeing on my infrequent trips across the state. Pittsburgh was not all steel mills and coal dust (how long had I been carrying *that* one around?). New Jersey was not all dilapidated housing, crumbling industry and mob influenced. Michigan was not all like Detroit, but Detroit was even worse than I had imagined. You get the drift.

So here I was, by preconception, in the home of coal mines, inbreeding and mountains on fire; miners and backwoodsmen, snake worshippers and unibombers. Somehow I missed them all.

* * * * *

Turns out West Virginia is a bustling, modern state with clean cities, well maintained roads, and good people. It was really, really green and clean, and the roads long and winding.

I stopped at memorials in Charleston, adjacent to the state capitol, West Logan and Bluefield. My host in Bluefield, Commander Bill Ascue of the local Legion post, invited me to dinner, and he and another veteran both sat for interviews.

Along the way I learned that not all service organizations at the post level, and that includes the American Legion, VFW, VVA or AmVets, are able or willing to be of assistance. Some that I located, through each of their proprietary databases, had been closed or disbanded, while others were still around but on life support through dwindling membership. Still others are just plain suspicious of strangers, however well intentioned, asking for aid or assistance.

Those who came through for me did it in a big way, and I hope I am expressing my gratitude appropriately in these pages. Thank you, Bill, for your help, your time, your generosity and your directions... they were right on.

The next day had me going crazy on many of those corkscrewing roads through western Virginia that included a stop at Drake's Branch before, continuing to Norfolk, my former home port.

I was blindsided by the memorial in Drake's Branch. The battle of the Ia Drang Valley in November of 1965 had been on my mind for a very long time. In researching another project a few years before, I learned about the shift in the thinking of Defense Secretary McNamara, a shift that would change our approach to the war and cause the decimation of a generation of American boys needlessly. But that is a subject for another time. It was also the subject of the book, *We Were Soldiers Once, and Young,* and the movie of the abbreviated name.

The small plot of land set aside for the memorial in Drake's Branch, set back from the road and hard to find, even for locals, contained a flagpole and a couple stone markers. On one of the markers was a list of seven names. At the top of the stone, one soldier was singled out in greater detail:

In memory of Gordon P Young
From Drakes Branch,
Army First Cavalry Division,
Killed in Action, Ia Drang Valley,
Republic of Vietnam
on 17 November, 1965

This was the first, and only, actual reference, that I would find, to the carnage that resulted from faulty intelligence; intel that allowed us to drop our boys into an LZ that was home to a 4000-man battalion of North Vietnamese regular army.

Back to the Tour. At this time Joseph Galloway, one of the authors of the book, was a Facebook friend of mine. I shared a photo of the memorial with him and got back more information about Gordon Young. It wasn't long after that Joseph and I parted ways over some online misunderstandings, but I will always be grateful to him for sharing with me and for putting a more human face on this long-ago event.

18. *July 10, 2013*

Norfolk, Virginia was a big surprise and a big disappointment to me. It had grown a lot in the more than forty years since I had been discharged (and promised myself *never* to return...oh well). I was hoping to get onto the base and visit the destroyer and submarine piers where my ship had been billeted. Well, I did and I didn't. Since 9/11, security at military installations has been tightened substantially. I was unable to get permission to go onto the base by myself, but I was able to pay for a bus tour of the base—no photographs, no getting off the bus—and had to settle for that. It was still worth it.

After an extra day (my first actual day off in six weeks) I headed north through eastern Virginia and for my second visit to the Holy Grail of Vietnam-specific memorials, The Wall in Washington DC.

I was invited into the home of the Director of United Charitable Programs, to stay during my three days in and around the nation's capital. Jan Ridgely and I had talked a hundred times, with me asking the same questions over and over and her patiently answering each and every time. But we had never met. It was a great leap of faith for her to invite me to stay, and one that I seriously appreciated. She and I and her S.O. Frank got along great. We shared a few meals and engaged in interesting conversation.

We even attended a wonderful concert in the front of a bicycle shop and basically interacted as old friends, which, in fact, we had become.

I also managed a visit to the WIMSA memorial in Arlington. This is one of the newer memorials in Washington and is dedicated to Women in Military Service to America. I was able to find records on their computer for both my mother's service as a WAVE in WWII, and my Aunt Lois, also a WAVE in the mid '50's. I recommend that anyone traveling to DC visit the memorial. It sits at the end of the Arlington Memorial Bridge Road, past the entrance to the Cemetery and just below the Lee mansion at the top of the hill.

During WWII women were accepted by all service branches as reserves. The WAVES were a naval reserve entity...it stood for Women Accepted for Volunteer Emergency Service.

Nearby Triangle, Virginia, is home to the Museum of the Marine Corps, just across the road from the Marine base at Quantico. In addition to the ultramodern and majestic museum building, there is a memorial walkway that celebrates the history of the Corps in a number of separate and discrete installations depicting all their major campaigns, including Vietnam.

Then, it was back to Jan's, packing up and heading north. These were a very civilized and necessary three days of peace and relaxation. As it turned out, they were the last I would experience for quite a while.

19. *Reflection*

So, now that I was little more than ten percent of the way through this adventure, how was I feeling, really?

Emotionally, I was somewhere else in this particular track and unsure of which direction the train is headed. Back in Denver I have lots of friends and acquaintances, especially at my home church, but it was hard to tell, while on the road, how many realize I'm even gone.

In truth, I have a hard time making really close friends, especially after my closest friend in the world stroked out and left this world about four years ago.

I know it is my responsibility to maintain my own world and my own attitudes, so, no excuses here, just a realization that I was a little more alone on the road than I expected to be. And the severe rain and thunderstorms the day before did not improve the mood.

I wasn't meeting the people on the road I had anticipated getting an opportunity to know. I expected to be interacting with more veterans along the way, especially since I was being supported largely by American Legion and VFW Posts. What I was getting is that they would just as soon make a reservation for me at a local hotel/motel, and direct me there rather than do a meet and greet at the local post.

And when I did get to spend time in a post with other vets, there tended to be a lot of silence, a lot of solitary smoking and drinking in groups that I was closed off from joining. I am of them, but, not one of them at the same time, and who was I to come around and stir up emotions and feelings?

And, personally, I don't smoke and hardly drink, and as a result, didn't fit in all that easily. It has been a real problem connecting.

When I stayed at a private home, especially those associated with my larger Church community, I had great visits, slept well, and upon leaving, reflected on the seeming perfection of their lives and spirits. These reflections only deepened and aggravated my own feelings of isolation.

But this was the road I chose. It was the path for which I had cajoled donations from a lot of friends and strangers, for which I planned extensively and upon which I still expected to meet a lot of incredible people before the end, in spite of appearances to the contrary. So, I kept on.

* * * * *

The next couple of days were a blur of Delaware, New Jersey and Maryland. My first destinations were some nicely done memorials in Dover and Newcastle, Delaware, followed by a memorable stop at Brandywine Park in Wilmington.

There are two memorials of note in the park. The first is the Vietnam Veterans' Memorial featuring a raised, rounded base on which stands a sculptured soldier cradling a wounded buddy in his arms. Nearby is a memorial to all black Medal of

Honor winners from all our campaigns. The hexagonal base contains brass plaques detailing who and when, and on top of the base stand cast bronzes of two black soldiers, one of WWII vintage and the other in a Civil War Uniform.

My home for a night in Wilmington, which I found on the internet where it looked and sounded really nice, turned out to be a dump of epic proportions, but I stuck it out. After I checked in (before seeing the room of course), I noticed gang-bangers, hookers and bugs all around the perimeter, but none of those made it into my room or my car. The next day I was off with the dawn.

My goal for the day was to travel all the way south to Cape May, New Jersey, several hours away, with a stop in Wildwood followed by a drive all the way back to Baltimore for the night.

Just on the west side of Cape May, the southernmost point of New Jersey, is Sunset Beach, home of Marvin Hume. Marvin is a WWII veteran who had been involved with our lost boys from Vietnam and other campaigns in a very different way. I pretty much begged his family to let me talk to him and get him on video. They called him and he agreed, and I was off on an adventure.

Marvin Hume enlisted in WWII along with two of his best friends, neither of whom survived the war. About 40 years before my visit, in the early '70's, Marvin bought the concessions at Sunset Beach. The outgoing owner had one unusual request. He raised the American Flag every morning during the season and took it down again at night. He wondered if Marvin would continue the tradition. Marvin agreed.

Shortly after, he took out an ad in a local paper asking if anyone had a casket flag they would like flown to honor their fallen loved one. The response was instantaneous and unceasing.

Over the last 40 plus years, Marvin has flown a different casket flag, donated by and returned to families of veterans of multiple campaigns, every day between Memorial Day and Veterans Day…thousands of flags. Marvin, at the time of our meeting, was 91 years of age. Legally blind, needing a walker to get around, and no longer taking an everyday part in the operations of his various businesses, he still gets out there each night for the flag lowering ceremony which attracts hundreds of spectators. He still has a two-year waiting list of flags to fly.

A succession plan with his family ensures that the tradition will live on once he is no longer able to do it. He is truly a gift of our time.

The way back took me to Wildwood, a small resort town on the eastern shore, north of Cape May. Veterans in the area built a full scale replica of The Wall on the end cap of a street fronting the beach. The catch was that the wall was longer than the end cap, and they solved the problem in a unique manner.

The wall is segmented from the panels in the center moving backwards, laterally, forward again on both sides, in a kind of "bat-wing" arrangement. It flows really well and is completely different from any other veterans' wall in the United States.

After paying $12.00 in tolls, three of them at four bucks a pop, to get from New Jersey all the way to Baltimore, I arrived at a reunion of sorts with my old friend, Scott Vermillion, and his wife, Angie. I had last seen them 10 years before at their wedding in Bath, New York, and had kept in touch only sporadically in the interim. Two kids later, three in all, catching up with each others' lives took a while. It was a great evening, talking about past friends and adventures. Then I pushed on westward through northern Maryland and into Pennsylvania when everything started to go haywire.

20. *July 20, 2013*

In my planning, I used what I thought was an intelligent methodology. I would arrange my soft landings and support ahead of time, but not too far ahead. The reason, I believed, was that too many things could happen—people forget, plans change, etc. So I planned the first seven weeks to a T, expecting that, as the days rolled on, I would be able to make my calls from the road and continuing to set up people and places while on the move.

Not so much. My days were full of driving, stopping at memorials, more driving, checking in where I had arranged to stay, visiting with hosts or writing my blogs and catching up/ filing photos, etc. Eventually I ran out of safe harbors and wound up taking it a day at a time.

My visit to Pittsburgh was one of those times. I had actually found a place to stay with a member of the local CSL church, but the host's plans changed and I was left essentially homeless. Options: pay for a motel room, sleep in my car or start begging through social media.

I posted on Facebook, got a couple of maybes, then saw a post from my sister to a friend of hers she knew was from Pittsburgh, but was currently out of the country. The friend knew someone there with a bed and breakfast who *might* be able to help. And she did. Katie Luckett was more than gracious to me and runs a beautifully maintained historic home as a B&B. I recommend the Mellor House to anyone desiring a warm welcome, charming stay and good memories. Thank you so much, Katie.

It was a great four night stay enabling me to visit the multiple memorials in the greater Pittsburgh area, check out some of the local restaurants, and vegg out just a little. The next day, a new friend and her grandson took me in tow and we did some sightseeing.

I had seen photos of the principal Vietnam Veterans' Memorial in Pittsburgh and couldn't wait to see it in person. Heading to the confluence of the three rivers (Allegheny, Monongahela and the Ohio), we moseyed along the river walk to the rounded cupola of the memorial and the unfolding of a very emotional experience. The canopy is suggestive of the Hibiscus pod, an eastern symbol of rebirth and regeneration, with hanging wind chimes signifying prayers for the dead. Inscriptions are in both English and Vietnamese and *"reflects the veterans' desire for peace, from war and from within themselves."*

Below the canopy are a series of life-sized sculptures, one of a returned soldier embracing his wife and child, and the others—a woman with arms outstretched beckoning to her son a few precious yards away, coming home from the war. As stoic as I tend to be and as adept at dealing with pain and other emotional contexts without allowing those emotions to take root inside me, I was moved to tears by the whole experience. And it wouldn't be the last time.

Knowing my next night was to be in Bedford, Pennsylvania, and knowing another B&B proprietor in Bedford, Katie gave me a glowing referral for Lynn and Steve at The Chancellor's House. It was another night well spent under the roof of a gracious couple who fed me an amazing breakfast the next morning on fine china, using Tiffany flatware. I had a lot of gratitude to express.

The rest of southern Pennsylvania went by quickly. Most of the memorials in that state were originals: small-to-medium sized installations outside the traditional stone marker and a flag near a courthouse. No memorial sites were any more or less memorable than any other, but I appreciated the diversity in design and execution this region offered.

And my reception in each city was also a little different. In Altoona, for example, the host post arranged for a hotel but not a meeting. And their memorial was spectacular...a half-sized reproduction of The Wall in DC, adjacent to the local VA Hospital. In Harrisburg, I was unable to secure lodging and would up with a room on my own dime. Philadelphia, on the other hand, was a completely different story.

On my way east I contacted one of my Facebook friends who had originally thought could host me, but was ultimately unable to comply. However, she contacted a friend at the local VA hospital, who knew someone in a veteran biker club who had a realtor buddy. He had a vacant house that might work. The vacant house did not work out but John and Carol Kustafik, the realtors in Downington who managed the property, invited me into their home for a couple of nights while I explored the greater area. John, I know you were Air Force in Vietnam, but Semper Fi anyway. On short notice you provided a miracle for me.

Downington itself, a town that hadn't been on my radar, had a very nice memorial that was supremely cared for on a daily basis. John's friend, Roger Paisley, designed and helped build the memorial, and spends part of each day of his life picking up loose trash, pulling weeds and kicking some butt when people don't respect the site, a kind of dedication not seen very often any more.

21. July 27, 2013

I arrived in New Jersey, driving right into Camden without a care in the world. Of course, I didn't learn until later that Camden is regarded as one of the more dangerous cities in the United States, but you couldn't have proven it to me that day.

I drove right down to the Waterfront where the USS New Jersey is moored, one of several battleships the navy has given to cities and states as floating museums. I was meeting Ron and Carol, members of a local American Legion post in Cherry Hills, who had offered to be my hosts for a couple of nights. I had the whole top of the house to myself, came and went as I pleased, and was able to visit a whole slew of memorials in the densely populated metro area while there. And I met a woman who was serving Vietnam vets in a totally new and unexpected way.

Sue Quinn-Morris is an example of someone who never served in the military but finds it important to support others who did, and has been involved in veteran-centric organizations since 2006. After joining the American Legion post in

Cherry Hill as an Auxiliary Member, her involvement shortly morphed into a labor of love known as The Dog Tag Project.

This project has reunited veterans and families of deceased veterans with dog tags lost in the jungles of Vietnam, artifacts that trigger massive memories in the minds of all involved.

Two New Jersey residents, approximately ten years apart, while visiting Vietnam, found hundreds of dog tags collected by a couple of Vietnamese scrap metal dealers. Sgt Fletcher's dog tag, whose story is detailed below, is one of the many that were turned over to State Senator James Beach, head of the New Jersey State Legislature's Veterans' Affairs Committee. And while there is more to tell about the chain of custody, they continued to be handed down till they wound up in Quinn-Morris' lap.

For the last several years she has been diligently working, researching, calling and mailing, trying to find the rightful owners of the dog tags. Although a small and somewhat tangential aspect of the aftermath of war, the effect on the recipients is often huge, which motivates her to do more, as illustrated in the following story.

> *May 12, 1968 in the village of Thua Thien, Republic of South Vietnam, Sgt Robert Melvin Fletcher was killed in action during the Tet Offensive.*
>
> *Wounded and bleeding out, he died in the arms of his closest buddy, far from home. His adoring cousin Darlene got the news just before Mother's Day that year. The friend, Sgt Clifford Searcy, survived the war, returned home, became a steel worker and eventually retired.*

Fast-forward more than forty years to a ceremony at VFW Post 1590, Daytona Beach, FL, where cousin Darlene watched Sgt. Fletcher's sister, Sharon Blais, receive a formerly lost dog tag from that friend Clifford Searcy and, for the first time, was able to hear from him about the final moments of her brother's life.

"I always thought of Robert's mother every Mothers Day," said Searcy. "You don't know how great a guy and what kind of soldier he was. He was not afraid. He was a good leader. And I was proud to have hold of him when he went."

"He did us justice. And because of guys like him, I am here to do this today."

After slipping the dog tag around her own neck, all Blais could say was, "Robert has come home."

Sue Quinn-Morris would be the first to tell you she doesn't do this alone. There are organizations she can call on to provide funding for the dog tag return ceremonies, as well as travel expenses for those involved. And the Nam Knights of America MC, a motorcycle club of Military and Law Enforcement professionals, are an integral part of her support system, transporting the dog tags and arranging logistics along the way. The precious artifacts are treated with honor and respect at all times.

* * * * *

I had been looking forward to meeting "Jarhead" Jim Ewen, a former Marine, who is doing something special for our guys and girls "over there."

Jim and his wife have a son, also a former Marine, who was deployed in the Middle East. From personal experience, while deployed aboard ship, I can attest to how well received care packages are to the soldiers and sailors far from home, and existing on whatever they are served.

Jim and his wife made a whole lot of beef jerky and sent it to their son. When the package arrived, all pungent and fragrant with the flavors of home, their son discovered more friends than he thought he had, all wanting to share in the booty from home.

Over time, Jim and his wife realized they couldn't keep doing it like they had been, trying to keep up with an ever increasing demand, and turned it into a business, Jim's Jarhead Jerky. Their "deal" is, for every box that is sold, they ship a box to a deployed soldier somewhere in the world for free.

It isn't about the money. It *is* about bringing a little bit of home to those that really need and deserve it. You can find Jim's Jarhead Jerky online or on Facebook, should you want to get some and support their efforts.

Jim: absolutely love what you are doing.

22. August 10, 2013

Restless after a few days in New Jersey, I moved into Manhattan for some interesting days and nights. I had a place to stay lined up, as a last resort, through Craig's List. Call me crazy, but if I was completely sane I probably wouldn't have ever begun this Tour. After scanning motels and hotels at $150-200 per night in the city, I found someone offering a couch in his apartment for only $50 a night. What a deal.

Turns out it was a single apartment in a high rise at 51st St and 10th Ave. There was no separate bedroom and only a sheet hung between his bed and my couch. Kind of cozy but it worked. I wasn't there that much, searching out memorials by day and enjoying the city by night. Parking was a breeze, taxis were handy and less expensive than I had imagined, and the days passed quickly.

The principal memorial in Manhattan is located just a block or so from the Staten Island Ferry terminal. It consists of a long wall made of translucent glass blocks, with quotations and the text of letters home from Vietnam, under the glass…there is also a brick walkway with kiosks offering more information about the war and its casualties. I was especially impressed and saddened by the profile of PFC Dan Bullock, a young man in every sense of the word, determined at 14 to find a way to enlist, and was trained and sent to Vietnam to die at 15…America's youngest casualty of the war.

> *The letters behind the glass, very ordinary and chatty, sharing complaints about the military, plans about the future, and doubts about the mission, in some respects all share a commonality. They were written by soldiers who were later killed in action. It wouldn't be the last time I would see this played out.*

When I had seen all there was for me to see for my own mission, I left Manhattan as fast as its roads would let me. I was headed to Long Island for a few surprisingly good days and saw some interesting installations, one incredibly stark memorial and another with as much emotional context as one can imagine. And I enjoyed a few nights in a kind of a commune in the middle of the island.

I never got as far east as the Hamptons, but I did get a taste of most of the island. Life slows to a crawl the moment you leave NYC proper—or perhaps that is just how it feels after the whirlwind that is Manhattan. The predominant feeling is freedom, the preeminent color is green and the primary scent is fresh and salty.

Outside of a couple of major freeways, most of the roads were small and very lightly traveled. They meandered through some exceptional country. From Queens to Huntington, Massapequa to Northport they were a joy to travel.

The living arrangement in Centerport wasn't a harkening back to the '60's-style commune, but a large house with a lot of space, and people of different backgrounds who were staying anywhere from a few days to a few months. It was luxurious in comparison to my stay in Manhattan. An intentional community, everyone got along well, interacted at a very high level and were big on sharing. In a word: fun.

The oddest and most striking memorial on Long Island is a stark and dramatic spire that rises smoothly and sharply above the native growth. Situated in Farmingville, Suffolk County, this white three-sided needle rises perhaps a hundred feet into the air, decorated only by a stylized American flag painted onto the spire, from the midpoint to the tip. Surrounded by a red guardrail, the memorial bears no placards of any kind to indicate its purpose. Only one small marker adjacent to the parking lot describes it as the Suffolk County Vietnam Veterans' Memorial.

The memorial that moved me the most was in East Meadow. Part of a large memorial park, and very hard to spot from the street, everything was symbolic. A flag-bordered walkway takes you back to the main part of the memorial grounds. There you are greeted by a pedestal marker for the POW/MIA's and a walk among rows of stone walls, each about waist high with names of the New York casualties of Vietnam.

Even the flowers planted along the walkway evoke the tragic roots of this park. In one area they are growing well and colorfully, with the exception of one dead plant, immediately evoking a memory of the "missing man formation" so common among military displays.

It is worth noting that among all fifty states, New York ranked in the top five in terms of number of the casualties attributed to Vietnam. Past the names, your breath is taken away at the sight of two stylized giant hands, about 20 feet tall, clasped together in an image of fright and anguish, and beneath them the simple inscription, *"All we ever had was each other."* A chain holding dog tags is stretched over the top hand of the sculpture. I had expected it, I'd seen photos of it in planning this journey, but I never anticipated the jolt through my body at the entirety of it. Unforgettable.

Done with Long Island, I headed west through Queens, skirting Manhattan; it was a couple hours drive to Port Jervis. Technically the town was still in New York, but go a block or two in any direction and you were in either Pennsylvania or New Jersey.

I met up with Mark and Maryann Cullen in Port Jervis, two of the most generous people I have ever met. Their service post is the aptly named VFW Tri-State Naval Ship Post, and I was given the grand tour before retiring to their home. They fed me and gave me a bed in, of all things, the 5th wheel mobile home in the driveway. At first it seemed pretty odd but it worked out very well. It had a king sized bed, electric and water hooked up to the house, and a workspace at the kitchen table so my being there wouldn't burden them. I tend to spread out wherever I am staying.

As I was preparing to head upstate, Mark offered to do any work I might need on my car, as he did all the routine stuff on his daughters' cars. I didn't need any help at the moment but that wouldn't last.

North through eastern New York, I cruised through West Point and Troy on the way to Albany and the home of another CSL minister, Rev. Joanne. While we were meeting for the first time, after dealing with each other over the phone, it turns out we had been long time Facebook friends through our involvement in the CSL community. She introduced me to a memorial in her city I hadn't known about, and I returned the favor one evening by chasing a bat out of her home. It seemed insane at the time, flailing away at this invading bat with a pillow from her sofa, trying to guide it back out the front door without injury, but it worked. Both were interesting, life affirming experiences.

After a few days in Albany it was time to head into western Massachusetts and Connecticut, where I was welcomed by Rev. Patrick Pollard and his lovely wife, who invited me to speak at his church in Middletown the following day. The Pollards turned out to be an interesting and engaging couple who, if we lived closer to each other on the planet, would have become great friends. I have fond memories of being in their home, breaking bread with them and watching a great movie before turning in. With his light and breezy Jamaican accent and quiet dignity, Rev. Patrick is quite the leader of his flock.

After the service, one of the members of the church approached me and asked, "Have you been to the memorial in Wallingford yet?"

Well, no, I had not even been aware of it. He said his brother's name was on the memorial and I really should see it. So we went. It was the first time for me to be at a memorial with a family member of a soldier memorialized thereon. It is also one of the few memorials I saw during the entire Tour that is positioned in the center of an intersection in a totally residential neighborhood…a quiet and beautiful space, and an absolutely unforgettable experience.

23. *August 24, 2013*

Moving out of Connecticut and into Rhode Island, I was eagerly anticipating a reunion with a childhood friend of my mother. I had last seen Anahid some thirty or so years ago on my last trip to the northeast, and her daughter, Dianna, slightly more recently on a long ago trip with friends to Los Angeles.

Rhode Island, our smallest state, contained several memorials. Through one of their friends (everyone knows everyone there, it seems), I was able to arrange some great interviews, including one with Tom Suprock, a former helicopter pilot in Vietnam. Tom flew what was known as a Loach, a Light Observation Helicopter.

For those unfamiliar with the Loach, it is something larger than the ubiquitous Bell helicopter with the all-encompassing bubble, yet with a lot of Lexan curved around the pilot for visibility. It is much smaller than a Huey, looking much like a drop of water on the wing, and more maneuverable, but not designed for a big payload.

Unlike the vast majority of Vietnam veterans I encountered on this journey, Tom was not only willing to speak about his adventures, but actively seeks out speaking opportunities in local high schools and colleges. And he does have a story to tell. In his words:

"The war was all about decisions, and decisions you had to make in an instant that would follow you for the rest of your life. My most difficult one was chasing down an aircraft that had been shot down in Cambodia.

"I was in my Loach, which is an OH-6A Cayuse. The civilian version would carry four people. We had two guys in it and we went down, and there were eight pilots getting off the aircraft. There was no way to get them all out, and the Khmer Rouge were coming out of the trees, the ones that had just shot them down.

"We took as much weight off the aircraft as we could, but I couldn't get eight people out in a four passenger aircraft. Turns out I could get light on the skids with five, which means three guys had to stay behind…there were going to be three dead Americans or ten dead Americans. And believe me, with the Khmer Rouge you were dead, but they would probably enjoy themselves for a while before you died.

"So, the decision was made that three couldn't get on, and since I was the aircraft commander, I had to choose which three people could not get on, and leaving people behind was something we never, never, ever did. We would never leave people behind. And for me to be forced into a decision like that was mind numbing.

"It haunts me to this day, and the faces of those three guys as I pointed at them it was like I was pointing a gun at them, and I looked down my finger at them as I pointed, and it was like I was holding a .45 on them and pulling the trigger, as though I virtually shot them and killed them myself. And I live with that to this day. Its, uh, quite a challenge.

"It is something that comes to me every night and something that will stay with me for the rest of my life. I sentenced those three men to death, my comrades in arms, because I just couldn't save them all."

Tom tells this story to students wherever he can. Not to frighten them or elevate himself, but to teach them the value of critical thinking, of making snap judgments for the greater good, and that decisions have consequences. In highly charged circumstances there are rarely good, clean endings. We all just go out there each day and do the best we can.

Somewhere between six and eight million young Americans served in and around Vietnam during those violent years. Many of them have tales to tell that are at least as violent and gripping of their psyches, but this was his, and I was privileged enough to hear it from him. Unfortunately, most of the veterans who have stories like Tom's, stories that could teach, transform and elevate minds won't talk about it.

Part of my mission was to meet some of these veterans, get them to open up, possibly to work with more of them on their issues related to PTSD and hypersensitivity, but I didn't get many chances while on the road. I'll never stop trying.

Through Tom and his friend Manoog Kaprielian (who introduced me to Tom) Rhode Island's vets have a couple of powerful advocates in their corner, and I was privileged to be able to meet them and get to know them a little.

* * * * *

A few days later I said goodbye to Anahid and Dianna and headed north and east into Massachusetts, home to perhaps more memorials per square mile than any other state.

John Beale, one of my Facebook friends, offered up his home in Abington, just south of Boston, and I spent a couple nights there. His house was small, and the only place he had for me was a little narrow couch that was just barely long enough for me to fit, but it was like manna from heaven to a starving pilgrim. His hospitality was, indeed, a gift.

> As things happen, more than a year before I left home, one of my Facebook friends in a Boston suburb, committed to hosting me for several nights. In the interim, he and his wife split up. She wanted nothing to do with him or any of his friends. I was temporarily homeless again until John stepped up.

That Sunday I had a chance to speak at the Boston CSL, a nice congregation led by two really energetic and capable licensed practitioners/ministerial students. I enjoyed the service and was able to put out a call for support that was graciously picked up by a member.

On my way to this member's home, I got a call from her that her daughter had just come home unexpectedly. Their home was no longer an option. I wound up spending the night in a local motel, and beat the drums for support once again through Facebook. Say what you like about Facebook, this faceless, oligarchic entity that just finds more ways to mess with its members than Carter has pills (you need to be of a certain age to get that reference), but the people who followed and supported me via Facebook were incredible.

When that didn't work and the shadows were getting longer, I called John again and he said just come on back. Got to say it wasn't the most ideal place to be, since he was south and the next few days would take me north of Boston and back down again, but it was snug and warm. John even took me around the area and showed me several memorials tucked away here and there that I had not found in my research. Through John, my days just got that much more fulfilling.

When it was time to leave for good I got a little emotional. Given what John had to give, I received more than my share and I was truly grateful…thank you brother.

Now I was in truly unexplored territory. I had been to Boston and points south a long time ago while researching another project, a historical footnote to the Civil War whose records were kept in the museum at Mystic Seaport in Connecticut. But I had never been farther north than the Boston suburbs.

It was not yet full on autumn, so the leaves hadn't begun changing. Despite the near continuous rain and damp the scenery was beyond spectacular.

24. *August 29, 2013*

North into New Hampshire, my first two stops were in Nashua, just above the Massachusetts state line. Deschenes Park in Nashua is a small slice of peace in the city, a park with the express purpose of honoring veterans from all our campaigns, nine in all, including a special wall honoring women who served: WAVES, WACS, Nurse Corps, WAF, and Spars. My mother would have been proud.

There is a tenth marker among the campaign markers with a simple inscription that reads, "Nine memorials here commemorate the great wars of our country. The tenth is for the war we hope we never have to fight." This stone was set sometime in 1999, obviously sometime before 9/11. More markers will need to be added sometime soon.

Heading farther north through the heart of New Hampshire is Woodstock, a quaint little city with a bustling and active citizenry, and outdoor businesses vying for tourist dollars alongside small bars and restaurants. I had to park off the main street and claw my way up a hill, in the rain, to photograph the town's memorial. The exercise was a breath of fresh air in a long day of travels.

Through a series of connections I managed to find shelter in the home of Ron "Pops" Reilly, a veteran and officer in his local service post. One of the nicest men I have ever met, Pops, who was actually about my age, took me to a fun Greek dinner at a local ethnic festival one evening, dinner with his son another night (my first experience with Lobster Mac), and a tour of the memorial on the campus of the University of New Hampshire in Durham. It has an indoor memorial in a room of the student center, and is quite colorful, reverential and bold.

I crossed into Maine the following day, passing a touristy attraction that boggled my mind. Up on a series of blocks, as if in dry dock, sat the USS Albacore, an early nuclear sub, much smaller than the boats that would follow it—more of a proof of concept, and very unexpected. The US nuclear fleet is purposefully kept so far and away from the public and the prying eyes of our enemies that its mere presence was startling. Oh well.

My principal mission in Maine was to visit the memorial adjacent to the state capitol in Augusta. I had seen photos of the memorial; a series of right triangles…stone pieces set in single file. They rested on the long side of the right angle with the hypotenuse off each soaring into the sky, the shortest in front and tallest in the rear. The central, darker stone had cutout silhouettes of two soldiers supporting a third, as if returning to base from a patrol. From the photos I expected the tallest piece to be about eight feet tall. Turns out in person, the cutouts alone are perhaps twice life-sized, with the whole installation soaring 25-30 feet into the air. It was a remarkable memorial and one that really puts the individual in perspective.

There were others in Maine; Rumford, Orono and Bangor, but none as thrilling and mesmerizing as the one on that field in Augusta.

I managed a couple of personal things while in Maine. The first was a visit with a former shipmate, Myron Elbrader, and his wife, catching up on the last forty-five years or so. How a good southern boy from Mountain Home, Arkansas, wound up in Maine is still a mystery. I also got a glimpse of the coastline in Waldoboro, thanks to my wonderful hostess Linda Betz, another CSL Practitioner and friend of Rev. Joanne in the Albany, New York area. After two restful nights in Waldoboro, that included a tour of the area and a historic lighthouse, and a lobster dinner on an old commercial pier, I was recharged and ready to cruise across Maine, through northern New Hampshire and into Vermont about a mile from the Canadian border.

A funny thing about that border; I'm not a terribly experienced international traveler, outside of my time in the Navy when a passport was not required. The last time I crossed into British Columbia, decades ago, on a ski charter, I made sure to have my birth certificate firmly placed in its own pouch in my duffel, intending to produce it for the agent while going through customs. Unfortunately, the bags all went into Canada before we did, and, while we could see the bags from where we were, they weren't accessible to us. For a while, no Canadian official would go the thirty or so feet to retrieve it without an act of Parliament. Eventually it got worked out.

Now, of course, you need a passport and, although I kind of knew it, I thought I'd give it a try anyway…just in case.

The only international border I've ever crossed by automobile was into Mexico several times in my much younger life. I was familiar with that border crossing. Canada was a different story. I turned north after seeing a sign that the border was less than a mile away. Closer and closer I drove. I finally got to the checkpoint I was expecting, planning to play a little dumb and ask if I had all the proper documentation, fully expecting to be turned away. Turns out, the joke was all on me.

The checkpoint was Canadian and I had driven approximately 100 yards into Canada before stopping. Without proper documentation I was already an international fugitive. The Canadian border guard was all smiles and wary eyes. After asking some very probing questions, and checking me against what I chose to believe were terrorist databases just to be sure, she allowed me to turn around and reenter the United States. I was home free, for about ten seconds.

After crossing back into US soil, I was stopped at the *American* border checkpoint. It was manned by a couple of male officers who weren't nearly as nice as their Canadian counterpart. Although I am an American citizen, I was held up because I didn't have the proper documentation to leave Canada. Go figure.

Just stay calm, answer politely, and do not let them know about the weapon in the car. Yeah, I was armed, more or less. Less, actually. I had borrowed a small handgun from a person or persons unknown prior to beginning this journey, knowing I would be driving into some strange and potentially dangerous places. I just never suspected a border crossing to be one of those.

The gun was resting, unloaded, in a locked box, under a couple hundred pounds of stuff at the rear of the passenger seat. In a real emergency it would have taken me about ten minutes to put it to any possible use.

After giving me one of those inspirational speeches that boils down to "What in the *freaking* world were you thinking?" or other words to that effect, the border guard raised the bar and I sailed back into freedom.

I never intended to get across that day, but since I would be at the top of the country for the foreseeable future, I thought it would be a good idea to check. Done, and done.

I could see Quebec Province from the highway and my cell reception was pinging off Canadian cell towers. I was getting radio stations in French and weirdly accented English (just kidding), but it might as well have been China for all its accessibility. Oh well…Vermont would have its own surprises.

25. *September 11, 2013*

Before entering Vermont I cruised through northern New Hampshire in search of a memorial in the city of Berlin. I knew of Berlin as the hometown of another shipmate from long ago. I tried off and on for nearly two years to locate Ron, but his family had no idea where he was or what he was doing. They thought California, perhaps, but it turned out to be a fruitless quest.

My route through Vermont basically followed a lazy "S," heading west to Enosburg falls and Franklin, south and east to Waterbury and Sharon, west to Rutland and back into northeastern New York. I stumbled upon the original home of Ben and Jerry's Ice Cream in Waterbury and stopped to take the tour and enjoy some wonderful free cups of the tasty treat at the end of the tour; kind of like the tour of the Coors Brewery in Golden, Colorado, but without the need of a designated driver.

Then, at a rest stop in Sharon, Vermont, came a bigger surprise. The entire rest stop was devoted to the Vietnam experience. There was a veritable museum, an honor roll and, off to the side built into the side of a hill, a wonderful multipurpose memorial. Erected in 1982, prior to the age of the Internet and easy research, it was billed as the first memorial in the country to our fallen soldiers sailors and airmen of Vietnam.

I hadn't the heart to tell them they were a decade and a half late for that honor, having already been to the memorial in Wentzville, Missouri, circa Deember, 1967. It was still quite a site.

My next stop in Rutland brought me to a much smaller and uniquely designed memorial. The centerpiece was a large block of marble laid out lengthwise. Like the sarcophagi in Europe that had figures carved in raised relief into the lid (think the Templar remains from *The Da Vinci Code*), this pure white block of marble held the sculpted image of a soldier in full battle dress, complete with helmet, in peaceful repose.

Then back into New York, past Fort Ticonderoga, over the Adirondacks and a pit stop in Ogdensburg, just across the river from Ontario Province.

* * * * *

Coming south through the fat eastern half of New York I passed through Fulton and Syracuse on the way to Utica, and a funky little house in Elmira that had been converted into a Vietnam War Museum. The veterans who operate it had amassed a collection of odds and ends that memorialized a lot of personal minutia of the day, and an impressive collection of uniforms.

I managed to trade one of my Tour hats for one of theirs, and they threw in a handmade scarf/muffler. I was touched at the generosity but was grateful for a completely selfish reason. My mother and sister have been actively contributing to Operation Gratitude for the last two or three years. Hand-knitting, between them, hundreds of similar scarves that are included in care packages that go out to active duty servicemen and women, veterans and families of vets, first responders and others. I liked it. I've included more about Operation Gratitude in a later chapter.

The next day took me north through Belmont, home of the famous stakes race, and on to Rochester and an encounter with a memorial that would cause me to briefly lose my mind.

I had secured lodging in Rochester in the home of a friend of a friend before heading out for a morning of promise, searching for the memorial I had seen only in small photographs. The pictures gave me an idea of what to expect, but I couldn't have been less prepared for what was there and how it would ultimately affect my life.

I found the park that housed the memorial and wandered through the parking lot till I found the path, a pretty straight shot to a clearing with a grouping of flagpoles with flags flying.

Off to the left was a descending path taking me to the lower level of the memorial garden. This path was lined with stainless steel bollards, about waist high and angled at the top. Each bollard represented one local serviceman killed in action. The angle at the top makes it easy to see the embedded disc representing each KIA's branch of service. The placard below the disc has the serviceman's name, dates of birth and death, and the local high school each attended. All of them lining the right side of the path in military precision, and they seemed to go on forever. Although there are only a little more than 280 bollards, their placement and the shape of the walk has the feel of a Mobius strip that just repeats on and on and on.

Friends and family members attach things to the bollards—photos, prayers and flags—personal things, proud things. The walk takes you past the Medal of Honor Grove and the Sculpture Garden, past a large loop in the path to the Garden of Reflection and, finally to the Learning Area. It was in the learning area that I completely lost it.

I need to go back a bit. I am a Practitioner of Religious Science, I have been on a particular spiritual path for nearly twenty years. Through study and practice we learn to deal with people and situations that are coming to us, with anything from a request for a prayer for a recently departed pet, or to say some words about a loved one who is currently facing a life challenge. Sometimes, the issues are theirs and come from a place of fear and anxiety so deep and so seemingly real that they forget the spiritual truth of their own being. We practitioners are trained to allow people to be themselves, to act out, to share their pain and grief without allowing it become ours as well. I started the Tour *knowing* I could handle it, knowing that the result of death and destruction I was headlong in pursuit of would be in my face every day, and acknowledging that it couldn't get to me; that I could help and heal without taking on the hurt and loss that was heaped upon me at every site.

One of my friends from church emailed me after reading some of my early posts and said, "Your heart must be breaking open." I wrote back saying, "nah, I'm okay."

I was wrong.

In the Learning Area there were several exhibits; large stone installations with facts, figures and quotes about the war. One stone held the names of nine men killed in Vietnam who, in spite of some of the very best record keeping in the history of record keeping, were unable to be buried in a hometown or last known city of residence, because the military had no record for them. The city of Rochester decided to adopt those nine soldiers, believing that no deceased veteran should remain truly homeless.

There was a poem on another stone entitled *Hello David* written purportedly by a nurse who served in Vietnam. It reads:

Hello David, my name is Dusty.
I'm your night nurse.
I will stay with you.
I will check your vitals every fifteen minutes.
I will document inevitability.
I will hang more blood
And give you something for the pain.
I will stay with you and I will touch your face.
Yes, of course I will write your mother
And tell her that you were brave.
I will write your mother
And tell her how much you loved her.
I will write your mother
And tell her to give your bratty kid sister
A big kiss and a hug.
What I will not tell her
Is that you were wasted.

I will stay with you and I will hold your hand.
I will stay with you
And watch your life flow through my fingers
Into my soul.
Goodbye David, my name is Dusty.
I am the last person you will see.
I am the last person you will touch.
I am the last person who will love you.
So long, David—my name is Dusty.
David—Who will give me something for my pain?

It was too much. I sat on a rock and cried, and cried for nearly an hour. I cried later when I read it to my host. I can feel my eyes beginning to water as I am writing this, even knowing today what I didn't know at the time, that the person who calls herself Dusty is a fraud; never a nurse, never served in the combat zone.

I cried because it spoke to my heart of a universal truth; that the cost of war is one of those actual trickle-down situations that no economists will ever speak of. That cost does not end with the final heartbeat of a soldier, but keeps making entries in the ledger of life, gathering interest against the souls of all who are touched by the soldier's death.

While I was sitting on that rock I came face to face with my own expression of faith. I began the Tour promising to do a Spiritual Mind Treatment or prayer for healing at each and every memorial I visited. And I had kept that promise. But I began to see how uneven my prayers had become: Long and lavishly worded at the larger installations, more brief and generic at many of the smaller memorials. I had forgotten, or pushed down, that each was in and of itself a sacred place. And every one of them, whether large or small, whether early in the day or at the end of a long day of travel and exertion, required my best effort, when all I wanted to do was find somewhere to hide away till morning.

I rededicated myself to doing better, doing my very best for myself, for the cities and towns I was passing through, for the families and friends of those represented in each memorial, knowing I would want the same were the roles reversed.

I came away from that memorial a very changed person.

And, finally, yes, Deanne, my heart was well and truly breaking open.

There is, in fact a 281st bollard, so poignant and so telling of the generation of Americans who served in Vietnam, that I feel compelled to include the text of the inscription here:

"This bollard is dedicated to all those men and women who lost their lives after Vietnam, because of Vietnam. To those who died from physical or emotional wounds and those who succumbed to death from their injuries, by their own hand, from cancer induced by Agent Orange, or substance abuse. It is also dedicated to all who continue to suffer after Vietnam from PTSD, pain, sleeplessness, anxiety, loneliness, rage, survivor guilt and/ or sadness. To their families who witnessed the suffering, shared the pain, but often could not understand. It is dedicated to all who picked up their lives, despite difficulties, and did their very best, contributing to America as they did with their service to country in Nam. Finally, this is dedicated to you who have come here today...you who loved us...supported us...remembered us...Thank you for quenching the thirst of our souls. May none of us ever again forget the cost of freedom and the sacrifices made. God Bless you one and all."

This theme would recur in other parts of the country in various ways, and I thank those citizens of the greater Rochester area who were able to break away from their various negative thoughts of the war itself to recognize and embrace the pain and angst of those who returned in body, if not in spirit.

A final word about Dusty: Sometime after the poem became part of the memorial landscape, the author was outed as a fraud. The poet, Dana "Dusty" Schuster, admitted the fraud at the same time admitting to psychological trauma that led her to the fraud.

But the sentiments ring genuine. I still feel the power behind the words. Tennyson wasn't at the Charge of the Light Brigade, or C.S. Forrester in the Napoleonic War, yet we still feel the strength and the reality inherent in their works.

This is how I see Hello David, as a faithful image of love and futility played out, God knows how many times, in those ugly years. There is an eternal truth in the words, if not their source. And, so, it is.

*　*　*　*　*

The rest of western New York was fairly uneventful. Modest memorials in Lockport, North Tonawanda and others were significant, yet less emotionally taxing after my experience in Rochester, and allowed me a little time to get myself back together.

Buffalo was unexpectedly charming and, being late September and not a month later, wasn't yet buried beneath three feet of snow (yes I've watched some late season football games in Buffalo from the comfort of my living room). And the harbor held massive toys for a former sailor. In addition to the memorial right at the waterfront, there was a squadron of museum ships: a cruiser, destroyer and diesel submarine, all of WWII vintage and available for exploration.

I took a side trip to Niagara Falls and saw some sights before heading south for Springville and Salamanca. Now, Salamanca is a very small town; the kind where everyone knows everything, so I asked around about the location of their memorial. More than once. Nobody knew. Finally, I found it about halfway down the three-block long Main Street, buried behind a couple of commercial buildings but in a very nice setting, open and green, right by the river that flowed along the edge of the town, respectfully designed, constructed and somehow, maintained. It angered me that it could be mostly forgotten in such a small city. Then again, part of my mission was to bring awareness to some of these lesser-known memorials.

26. September 24, 2013

Driving due west had me skirting Lake Erie into Pennsylvania for the last time, for visits to memorials in Erie, Clarion and Fredonia, then once more into Ohio for the Buckeye State's northern memorials.

After a couple of stops in northeastern Ohio, toward New Philadelphia and Dover, home to another shipmate, Jim Hershberger. I had only sporadic contact with him over the years. We managed to have a nice conversation in their home. I took a few photos and I was on my way north again to Clinton, Home to a statue that has thrilled and haunted me since the day I discovered it online.

My reception in Clinton was amazing. Not only was I expected, but I was celebrated, thanks to the wonderful team that takes exceptional pride in what they have created. It is an amazing memorial park of about three acres with multiple exhibits, all having to do with the Vietnam experience.

As soon as you exit your car you are walking around, through and over memorial plaques placed by organizations and military units from all over. The brick path takes you to their "Wall," a long, low rectangular edifice that stretches a full 225 feet and contains the names of the more than 5000 dead from the state of Ohio on one side, and images from the war on the other.

Facing the wall is a statue to the Gold Star Mother, carved exquisitely from granite...a serene image of a woman at peace, for the moment, with the immensity of her loss, clutching the casket flag to her chest. That statue alone had drawn me here, little by little, for nearly four years.

The Gold Star Mother is an iconic figure in American military history, a symbol of acceptance of sacrifice and duty borne by mothers of every campaign. Two graphic examples were represented in Steven Spielberg's incredible movie Saving Private Ryan, when Mrs. Ryan sees the uniforms exit their automobile, recognizing them for what they were: emissaries of grief. And, moments before with the reading of that sad, sensitive letter to a civil war era mother, informing her of the deaths of her sons. I saw several representations of the Gold Star Mother on my journey, some including the children left behind, and they never failed to move me.

Off to one side sits a Cobra attack helicopter, on a pedestal about 15 feet off the ground in attack mode, all painted up and bristling with "armaments."

Obviously, the federal government was not going to give away something like a working aircraft with live weapon systems, so the caretakers/creators of the site found some components at Home Depot, screwed them in place, painted them and the result looked real enough for display purposes.

At the other end of the wall sits a rocky stream that ends in a reflecting pool. The water has been dyed black in honor of the POW/MIA corps.

And scattered throughout the park are benches dedicated to the memory of various departed souls. One in particular to Sharon Lane, the first nurse in Vietnam to be killed in a hostile action.

There are other displays planned: the addition of a Huey, a statue of the Gold Star Father and others, in this meticulously maintained memorial garden.

From Clinton it was onward and northward through Seville, Medina, New London and Amherst, with an overnight rest in Cleveland. It was near the end of September. I had been on the road for almost four months and had visited slightly more than 300 memorials.

* * * * *

Cleveland was an unexpected pleasure. I arrived early on a Sunday morning, planning on spending the day but with no real anchor or safe harbor set up. All my contacts in the area flamed out and I was left on my own. So, I went to church. Reverend June Clark at the Miracle Center for Spiritual Living had no idea who I was or what I was doing there, but she greeted me with open arms and a huge smile. I explained what I was doing, my affiliation with the Mile Hi Church in Denver, and requested that I be able to make a brief announcement during the service. She was only too happy to oblige.

I addressed the congregation and laid out my need for shelter that evening. Hank Lawson, one of Rev. June's practitioner students, offered up he and his wife's home for the evening. It wound up being there two nights and I was in heaven: home cooking like I hadn't had in months— real comfort food, and a bed as unlike a motel bed as it is possible to be. Hank and I drove into Cleveland together to visit its memorial and he was kind enough to show me around the area, especially Twinsburg, the 'burb they lived in; a city with an interesting set of founders.

> Moses and Aaron Wilcox were identical twins who lived together in the early 1800's, married sisters, died of the same disease on the same day, and were buried in the same grave. Not a story you hear often but what is travel without a little historical perspective. The town currently holds an annual festival for twins, but non-twins are also welcome. Beginning in 1976 with 36 sets of twins, the festival has grown to include around 3,000 attending pairs.

East and a little south brought me through Indianapolis and on to St. Louis, where I would board a plane to Los Angeles for a break. It was time for my 50th high school reunion, and I planned to spend a little time with other friends and family before flying back a week later and resuming the journey.

* * * * *

This seemed like a good time to take a physical inventory. At this point in the Tour, a number of things were happening to me at once. Arthritis had begun asserting itself on my system. I have joked in the past that if my right side was like my left, I'd be running marathons, but if my left side was like my right, I'd be in a wheelchair. Neither of those statements is absolutely true but, while my left side is virtually problem free, I have issues with nearly all my major joints on the right. The person who rear-ended my car in 2011 didn't do me any favors.

Confined to my vehicle for hours on end and sleeping on a succession of strange beds was no real help either, but I had to admit, the only times I could swear to being absolutely pain free and comfortable was behind the wheel.

But now, about four months into the journey, my knees were becoming problematic; fine while driving, but any journey longer than thirty minutes would find me exiting the car gingerly and holding on for about thirty seconds. As my knees became acclimated to holding my weight, I could begin to walk again comfortably. A condition I've come to know as a symptom of osteoarthritis. Suck it up and keep on truckin' as we used to say in the '60's.

My weight, while a little elevated for several years, had been relatively stable. One of my concerns starting this journey was that I would not be able to control the weight. I've heard tales of long-haul truckers ballooning behind the wheel on a diet of popcorn, potato chips and soft drinks. I actually did an intentional weight loss regimen in the days and weeks leading up to the start of the Tour that helped, and I finished the trip only slightly above where I began. It was difficult but not impossible to make some decent food choices along the way.

In the back of my mind always was the image of my stepfather, 93 at the time of the Tour, losing his mobility by inches, and seeing his life limited to not much more than his bedroom, bathroom, doctor visit and the occasional haircut out of the home. I was determined that would not happen to me, and at the age of 67, I recognized the need to be careful.

Stress was not a major part of my days on the road, the Rochester experience aside. At my high school reunion I connected with one of my classmates whom I hadn't seen in fifty years. That connection led to many long calming nighttime conversations in the coming months and helped keep me reasonably sane. Thank you, Claudia. I also reconnected with other classmates who had relocated around the country. A few of them were able to offer various means of support over the course of the rest of the journey.

All in all, I was pretty much where I expected to be physically, despite the issue with the knees. About three months later even that issue would be helped somewhat. More about that farther along in this story.

I'd like to take a moment and acknowledge the assistance I received from Tony and Brelinda in O'Fallon, IL. At a time when I needed shelter for an extended period of time, these strangers, Tamara's sister and brother in law, allowed me a full week in their home. It was enough time to get some needed work done on my Tourmobile, and revise the rest of the itinerary one more time. They fed me, spent time with me, and even lent me Tony's Cardinals jersey so I could take Tamara to another Cardinals baseball game, one day before the end of the season. What a blessing they all were to me and my cause.

27. October 3, 2013

I landed in St. Louis, got back in the Tourmobile, and headed to Indianapolis to begin the next part of the Tour.

This time through I was able to spend a little time in Indy, including a night in a motel next to the Speedway, and a visit to the memorial downtown: a towering half cylinder with some meaningful reminders of the war on the convex side, and letters home from Vietnam engraved in the stone on the concave side.

From Indianapolis it was a journey north and east through Noblesville, Muncie, Marion (home of two fine Vietnam specific memorials), Columbia City and Auburn, on my way into Michigan.

Michigan was not nearly what I expected. I had last been there about ten years previous on an overnight business trip to Troy, and before that when I was about two years of age. All I had heard recently was about the decline of Detroit, and I pretty much expected the entire state of Michigan to be a pretty impoverished place. I couldn't have been more wrong.

Well, Detroit lived down to my expectations but the rest of the state was magnificent.

I spent some time visiting memorials in many of the Detroit suburbs including Ypsilanti, Westland, Hazel Park, Garden City, East Pointe, Ecorse, River Rouge and Novi. It was easy to spot the city limits of neighboring Detroit. When I ran out of gutted, burned out buildings and fenced blight, I knew I was out of Detroit proper. I remember passing a business called Roy's Rib Cage that had been closed, vandalized and gutted down to the building's own ribs, visible from the street as I drove by.

I was very happy to leave Detroit and head to Lansing, the state capitol, and home of the Michigan Vietnam Veterans' Memorial. It is a sprawling and lovely memorial within the state capitol complex. Unfortunately, the memorial was undergoing some reconstruction at the time, and I was unable to photograph much of it without evidence of the construction. Beautifully laid out and built, it is a jewel among Vietnam-specific memorials all over the country.

Journeying farther north through Saginaw, Bay City and Mount Pleasant I came to the little town of Coleman, and a very different and memorable experience.

Coleman's tribute, while multigenerational and covering the conflicts of the last seventy years was extremely touching. The centerpiece of the memorial is a group of five statues all facing the "Soldier's Cross." The closest figures, bronze in color and representing those fighting the global war on terror, were a male and a female combat soldier...the only female in a combat role I can recall seeing on the entire Tour; helmets off in reverence to the symbolic battlefield altar. Behind them are three grayed out figures of men representing the spirits of those who fell fighting in WWII, Korea and Vietnam. The genesis of the memorial was a Vietnam veteran by the name of Randy Zylman whose son, Casey, was killed serving in Operation Iraqi Freedom. A committee was formed and the memorial is the result.

The park is full of maple trees, which were shedding their seed pods at the time. I had never seen one of these maple "airplanes" before and had to ask a local resident what they were. These airborne seed pods have evolved with "wings" that allow the pods to sail on a breeze as far as they can to begin a new life without crowding out the old growth; truly, a metaphor for the ongoing spread of life.

Still farther north, to the memorial in Cheboygan, and overnight in probably the most beautiful little town I've ever seen, Mackinaw City. The legion post there was happy to support my efforts, and I was able to travel around this incredible place, from the waterfront in the old part of town to the foot of the massive bridge that connects the main body of Michigan to the Upper Peninsula, all of it pristine and clean and like a large picture postcard. Of course this was early October and I imagine it looked far different a month or so later with the onset of winter.

The next day I headed south and west with my first stop in Petoskey, listening to some classic Bob Seeger in my CD player, which ironically included a lyric about leaving Mackinaw City. In Petosky, I learned that Seeger has a home nearby and spends a lot of his off tour time in northern Michigan.

Grand Rapids was a big disappointment. I was there during the very brief time our government was shut down, and was unable to access the Gerald Ford Library and Museum. The museum reportedly has an exhibit of part of the former US embassy in Saigon that I was hoping to see, but was rebuffed.

Completing a long day of travel I pointed the car west to Lake Michigan at Muskegon, south through St. Joseph and on into Indiana for the last time.

* * * * *

Some people don't seem to wander too far from the nest during their lives. One of these is my old friend and shipmate, Jim O'Brien, born and raised in Elkhart, Indiana, and still there. He and I had a few adventures in places around the world, but the clearest memory I have is of the two of us in Washington DC sometime in the late '60's. We were in DC wandering around the Washington Monument and decided in the moment to take the stairs to the top, not walking, but running. I was in much better shape at the time, truth be told. And we had probably been drinking, just a little.

So up we went in civvies and leather shoes, up and around all 990 steps, ninety-nine flights of ten, and finally, collapsing at the top, rolling around on the platform totally spent and causing other tourists to jump over our bodies to move around. Like life, there wasn't much room at the top.

Fast forwarding nearly fifty years, we had a nice visit. Then I was on my way farther west through Michigan City, Munster, Leroy and La Porte, on my way to a very unexpected find.

Just across the state line in Calumet City, Illinois, I had to really hunt for a very small but significant memorial. Not much bigger than a breadbox, somewhat overgrown and flanked by a thin grouping of flagpoles is a small marker dedicated to veterans of both Korea and Vietnam. It is dated May 30, 1967, making it the earliest in the nation to honor Vietnam veterans, dedicated about six months prior to the dedication of the memorial in Wentzville, Missouri.

* * * * *

I headed north into Wisconsin and a stay with another of my Facebook friends, Mark Kramer, in Green Lake. Mark, a former soldier in the Army's 25th infantry division, was an incredible help to me. Not only did he give me shelter at a time when I really needed more than being alone again in an anonymous room in a forgettable motel, he also set up two speaking opportunities for me, the first was in a local VFW Post, and the second at the University of Wisconsin in Oshkosh. It was the first time I had ever seen my name, in lights on a marquee. I spoke to a small but enthusiastic audience that night. From Mark's home I was able to travel quite a distance to visit Milwaukee, Neshkoro and Two Rivers in Wisconsin, and all the way up to Iron Mountain in the far western part of Michigan's Upper Peninsula, just over the Wisconsin state line.

Iron Mountain was magnificent. The memorial was part of an elaborate memorial park an open-air plaza in a corner of the local ski area. It was actually perched on the edge of the drop off that became the landing area of the ski jump at the resort. I was able to walk into the bottom of the snowless ski jump for a couple photos…the only way I will *ever* get on a ski jump. Being the middle of October, the seasonal change was starkly evident, and looking out over the natural valley to the forested rise on the other side, seeing a hundred shades of yellow, brown and orange was a genuine blessing to me, and one of the most beautiful vistas I saw all year.

One night during my stay with Mark we had dinner with one of his veteran buddies, Ray Hudzinski, a member of the Army's 101st Airborne in Vietnam. We spent a couple hours with a high school student being interviewed for a school project. Another night we played cribbage with a local club. Altogether a very satisfying visit. Thank you, Mark, for helping me relax and recoup. Then I was off for an entirely new and unique experience.

* * * * *

Neillsville, Wisconsin, is the home of the High Ground, a vast memorial park devoted to the Vietnam experience. The sprawling grounds of the memorial complex, with its multiple exhibits and open spaces, is the largest I would see all year. The centerpiece of the park is a larger than life sculpture dedicated to the Native American veteran. It is surrounded by reflective and meditative areas, and a sculpture garden with a set of bronze figures representing a mother with child, telegram in hand, and all that implies…fountains and hiking trails as far as the eye can see, and more than I can put into words. After The Wall in Washington DC, the High Ground should be on every Vietnam veteran's bucket list.

After the High Ground, the plan was to go generally west through Minneapolis/St. Paul and north to Duluth at the westernmost tip of Lake Superior, the only Great Lake I had not yet seen. But as I was pulling into St. Paul, Mother Nature brought the first storm of the winter in from Canada and shut down most of northern Minnesota. This was only mid-October. Part of my research in developing the Tour was extensive planning and plotting from almanac-based weather patterns and I was not expecting snow quite this early.

The really bad news: the itinerary for the next three weeks was to travel through Iowa, the Dakotas, Montana, Idaho and eastern Washington State. Now, most of that was not going to happen.

The December prior to the start of the Tour, I made a practice run through some western states. I drove from Denver to Los Angeles to spend the holidays with my family, and, on the return trip, visited memorials in southern Nevada and throughout Utah. A big snowfall in Utah the day before I started back showed me the folly of slogging through winter weather. The driving was more difficult, the memorials were affected by the snow, creating blinding glare and making them hard to photograph effectively, diluting their impact.

So, thinking quickly, I spent an extra day in Minneapolis revising the itinerary once again. The new route took me south and east into Iowa, through Nebraska again and home to Denver for a little R&R. I would have time to clear up some loose ends that had come up along the way. I managed to spend the time with my good friend Lee Cucinella who allowed me the use of a spare bed in her home, some really good home cooking, and the freedom to take care of that which needed attention. The Dakotas could wait for another day.

Nearly five months to the day I left, I was back in Denver having completed the first half of the journey.

Memorial Park, Winfield, KS: Modeled after "The Wall," well executed and maintained in a natural bowl.

Vietnam Veterans Park, Kansas City, KS: An entire city block of fountains, and displays in the heart of Kansas City—walkways for meditation and reflection as well as a wall of remembrance dominate the park.

Mark Twain Lake, Missouri: An incredibly beautiful and inspiring setting. This memorial sundial casts its shadow on each of the 12 markers surrounding it, each stone bearing the names of local youths felled in battle, during the appropriate month of each year. Note the simple soldier's cross at the foot of the gnomon.

Fireman's Park, Wentzville, MO: Dedicated in late 1967, this simple column topped with a stylized eagle, is one of the earliest memorials in the nation to those who fought and died in Vietnam.

Ohio Veterans Memorial Park, Clinton, OH:
A magnificent rendering of the archetypal Gold Star
Mother, calm and stoic in the face of her personal
tragedy, clutching all that remains of her previous life.

Ohio Veterans Memorial Park, Clinton, OH: Profile of the statue. The bench, to the left of the statue's base is a tribute to 1st Lt Sharon Lane, the only nurse to fall from enemy fire in Viietnam, 8 June, 1969.

Ohio Veterans Memorial Park, Clinton, OH:
The 225 foot long wall of remembrance that dominates the park.
The sheer power of seeing more than 5000 names of Ohio's KIAs
has overwhelmed the visitors in the photo.

Vietnam Veterans National Art Museum, Chicago, IL: Curator Joe Fornelli, pictured, is a Vietnam Veteran. He and other founding partners have created a space to display artwork and artifacts created from the pain and passion of other veterans.

Vietnam Veterans National Art Museum, Chicago, IL: One of approximately 2,500 pieces in the museum's rotating inventory.

Vietnam Veterans National Art Museum, Chicago, IL:
A display of artifacts primarily used by the Viet Cong
and NVA during the war.

Wabash Plaza, Chicago, IL: Placed below street level and fronting the Chicago River is this peaceful and respectful installation in honor of Chicago's lost sons.

Lansing Municipal Airport, Lansing, IL: A remarkable memorial in a forgotten location, much like our history in Viietnam.

Lansing Municipal Airport, Lansing, IL: Detail of the magnificent wall below the "Hovering" Huey, seen and appreciated by very few.

Columbus Park, Wildwood, NJ: A 60% replica of "The Wall" facing directly on the Atlantic Ocean, shoehorned into a smaller footprint and utilizing a unique "Batwing" design to fill the end cap of a residential street.

North Shore Trail, Pittsburgh, PA: Underneath this stylized Hibiscus pod, the eastern symbol for rebirth and renewal, two families come together again. A husband and father to his wife and child, and a son to his mother.

North Shore Trail, Pittsburgh, PA: The culmination of a year of a soldier's duty and courage, and a mother's fear and sacrifice.

Vietnam Veterans Memorial Plaza, New York, NY: Near the Staten Island Ferry landing at the tip of Manhattan is this amazing glass block structure, the centerpiece of New York's tribute to its veterans.

Vietnam Veterans Memorial Plaza, New York, NY: This walkway adjacent to the glass wall hosts several kiosks, each with additional information about the Vietnam War.

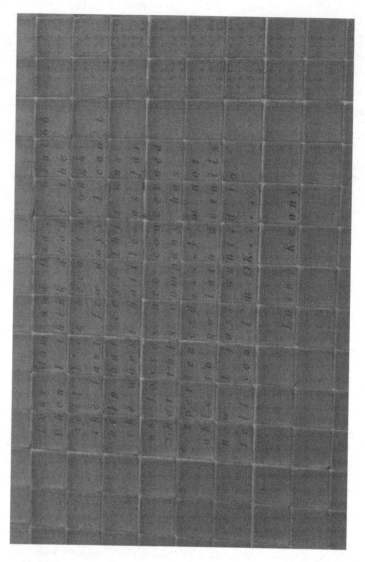

Vietnam Veterans Memorial Plaza, New York, NY: One of several letters home, embedded in the glass block wall, from native New Yorkers who never made it back alive from Vietnam.

Eisenhower Park, East Meadow, NY: Vast sprawling memorial park honoring veterans of all campaigns with individual segments.

Eisenhower Park, East Meadow, NY: A tribute to the brotherhood among our fighting forces in Vietnam… a tortured grip connecting two souls in battle.

Eisenhower Park, East Meadow, NY: A closer look at the detail...the pain and the energy behind the creation of this amazing sculpture.

Capitol Park, Augusta, ME: A soaring tribute to our men in battle and the care they took of each other front and center in the brilliant cut-away section of the center panel.

Capitol Park, Augusta, ME: The author behind the cut-out to give a proper sense of the sheer power and scale of this memorial.

Highland Park, Rochester, NY: A memorial so vast it requires a map to guide you through the intensely emotional landscape of this remarkable space.

Highland Park, Rochester, NY: A steady march of the dead in the form of stainless steel posts, with military precision, marking the path. Each post represents one fallen soldier from the greater Rochester area.

Highland Park, Rochester, NY: Most likely a family member added a little personal memento of their soldier kin, a way of saying he was more than just a memory...still alive in their hearts and minds.

Welcome Home Our Truly Homeless Veterans

On the Vietnam Veterans Memorial Wall in Washington, D.C. are the names of nine men whom the government has no record of their places of birth, nor of their home towns. These remain truly homeless veterans. With the dedication of this memorial on September 8, 1996, Rochester, New York veterans adopt these nine men, who were killed in action on the date listed. Welcome home, our brothers.

Clark T. Boots	October 3, 1970	Randall K. Sweertz	Date unknown
Peter B. Brown	October 10, 1966	Frankie Northern	September 8, 1970
Michael R. Haliburton	August 8, 1970	Michael P. Ribich	April 12, 1969
Christopher S. Miraslia	September 3, 1970	Francis M. Rinker	April 9, 1967
John O. Nary	December 20, 1968		

Highland Park, Rochester, NY: An amazing gesture by the community for a group of our soldiers that deserve to be remembered and honored by someone, somewhere, for their sacrifice.

Coleman, MI: A memorial depicting reverence for duty and service among generations of veterans. Forward figures are praying before a soldier's cross while the spirits of the dead (the lighter hues of bronze) offer their support.

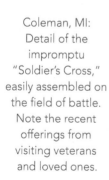

Coleman, MI: Detail of the impromptu "Soldier's Cross," easily assembled on the field of battle. Note the recent offerings from visiting veterans and loved ones.

DEDICATED TO THE VETERANS
OF
KOREA AND VIET NAM

GOLD COAST MANOR IMPROVEMENT ASSOCIATION

MAY 30 1967

Roadside display, Calumet City, IL: The earliest known memorial to our involvement in Vietnam, established in May of 1967, likely designed by a career soldier who served in both campaigns. The breadbox sized marker sits in a small grove surrounded by three flagpoles.

The High Ground, Neillsville, WI: A huge meandering collection. of exhibits commemorating many aspects of the Vietnam War. This is the only tribute to the Native American Veteran encountered on the Tour.

The High Ground, Neillsville, WI: A gripping and wrenching work of art picturing men in extremis on the battlefield. The metal "feathers" hanging beneath and behind the caped figure are each inscribed with the name of a fallen soldier.

The High Ground, Neillsville, WI: The sculpted image of shock and uncertainty in the faces of a young mother/widow, holding the folded casket flag of her husband, and her child holding on for dear life, knowing everything is different and not understanding why.

Capitol Grounds, Salt Lake City, UT: A beautifully crafted memorial virtually in the shadow of the state capitol building.

Capitol Grounds, Salt Lake City, UT: A detailed look at the larger than life statue of a warrior returning from a patrol with the proverbial "Thousand Yard Stare," looking at everything and nothing, having seen too much and experienced too much to adequately process in the moment.

Capitol Grounds, Olympia, WA: The edge of the memorial in downtown Olympia featuring a graphic cut away of both North and South Vietnam. A virtual crack in the wall, symbolic of the great forces that opened fissures in our national psyche during the war.

Washington Park, Portland, OR: A slow walk along the pathway to the Garden of Solace, the starting point in this huge, spiraling memorial.

Washington Park, Portland, OR: From the overpass that completes the first loop of this large urban bowl. Each of the smaller structures in the distance tells the story of two years of wartime both at home and abroad.

Washington Park, Portland, OR: My friend, also a Vietnam era veteran, in front of the stele marking 1966-67. Along the top is news of the day in Oregon and Vietnam, and below, the names of those lost of Oregon's contribution to the war effort.

Washington Park, Portland, OR: A close up of this stele, covering 1966-67, reveals not only the cost of the war in terms of the number of casualties Oregon suffered, but also the mood of the day back home.

On land, at sea, and in the air, the U.S. greatly increased its offensive against North Vietnam. U.S. troops numbered nearly half a million, using two thousand tactical aircraft and dropping two million tons of bombs. This massive offensive prevented the fall of South Vietnam but did not defeat the North Vietnamese, who withstood the bombing and increased their infiltration of South Vietnam. The cost to the U.S. was high: an average of a thousand and more Americans killed each month. This led to increased opposition to the war at home. In the Congress Senator Wayne Morse of Oregon, in the streets of the nation's capital the 200,000 who marched for peace.

FRED J. WILLIAMS JR.	RICHARD P MC STRAVICK JR.	DONALD G. MILLER	GERALD D. HUFFMAN	KENNETH C. HURSE
CHARLES L. ROBERTS	HERB DOBY	JAMES W. FOSTER	LEWIS C. COOK	HUBERT C. VAN POLL
WALTER R. SPEARE III	KENT L. JOHNSTONE	GARY W. MARTINI	KENNETH D. PHARES	CHARLES H. SNOW
JIMMY S. DAFFRON	VICTOR V. ULLBERG	KIT BLACKWELDER	LELAND H. THOMPSON	JOE C. LEUTENEGGER
EUGENE B. RHOADES	GERD F. SEELIG	RONALD L. BARBER	DALE W. TOLBERT	THOMAS J. JONES
LLOYD H. ROHDE	MAXIMO YABES	BRADLEY A. NELSON	CLIFFORD L. MENZIES JR.	ARTHUR A. ERWIN
DERALD D. SWIFT	DOUGLAS O. MUNDHENKE	RONALD H. JOHNSON	GEORGE N. WRIGHT	DANIEL F DE BUTTS
ERIC A. BRANNFORS	WILLIAM H. KOHO	JOHN F. FLEMING	JAMES W. CARTWRIGHT	CHARLES L. MOORE
	GENE W. GOEDEN	MONTY D. BUTTON		

Capitol Grounds, Sacramento, CA: This is a truly expansive memorial with a footprint larger than most, depicting scenes that I wouldn't see anywhere else on my journey. Remembrance panels cover the exterior.

Capitol Grounds, Sacramanto, CA: A soldier at rest, reading a letter from home and thinking about "The World" that he barely remembers.

Capitol Grounds, Sacramento, CA: Sculpted image of a
frustrated doctor working on a mortally wounded warrior.

Capitol Grounds, Sacramento, CA: Sculpted image of a prisoner of war in his bare cell in the Hanoi Hilton. This memorial had much more to offer a visitor.

Veterans Home, Yountville, CA: One of the most emotional of the tour on many levels. Note the small hands at the bottom right, unwilling to let go of either parent in the moment.

Coronado Naval Station, Coronado Island, CA: The US Navy/
Coast Guard memorial and tribute to the Riverine craft used in Vietnam.

Coronado Naval Station, Coronado Island, CA: An intensely visual
display of three types of river craft used by the US Navy in the
Mekong delta, beautifully maintained and detailed.

Coronado Naval Station, Coronado Island, CA: A tribute to those lost in Operation Game Warden, a little known effort to deny the Viet Cong use of the river ports of the Mekong delta.

Venice Beach, CA: An anonymously produced list on all POW/MIAs
of the Vietnam War painted on a long wall, part of a public works
depot along a major thoroughfare a block from the beach.

Venice Beach, CA: A look at the unfortunate aspects of age
and neglect affecting an otherwise bold and emotional
memorial, not to mention the vandalism and graffiti
found around the edges of the wall.

Angel Fire, NM: This memorial, now operated by the DAV,
showcases the ability of one man to change the landscape forever.
Built by a local doctor in memory of his son who was KIA in Vietnam,
it has grown beyond its initial footprint to be a gathering place for
veterans of all stripes, not just the disabled.

Angel Fire, NM: One of the many exhibits in the memorial, worn smooth by the touch of many hands over the years.

Angel Fire, NM: Some of the many offerings left behind by visitors to Angel Fire, the stones perpetuating a tradition that now transcends faith and nationality.

Battleship Park, Mobile, AL: A father, uncle or brother honors the memory of a loved one inscribed into the wall, with the superstructure of the mighty USS Alabama, BB-60, in the background.

Battleship Park, Mobile, AL: Holding tightly to the last symbol of his departed hero's sacrifice.

Patriot's Point, South Carolina: A glimpse of life "In Country" for those who didn't have the "Privilege" of being there, this mock support base shows us how our sailors lived and the conditions under which they served.

Vietnam Veterans Memorial, Washington, DC: Veterans and late spring visitors from all over the United States and around the world. It is the most visited site in the nation's capitol.

Vietnam Veterans Memorial, Washington, DC: Uncle, grandfather or family friend? The Wall touches generations of Americans

Vietnam Veterans Memorial, Washington, DC:
My high school friend, Clifford J Volke II, KIA 23 Jan, 1968,
not quite 22 years of age. His voice, his solid friendship and love
of life suddenly stilled forever nearly a half century ago.

*Visit my website to see these
photos and more in full color at
www.bruceacampbell.net*

28. *November 10, 2013*

Leaving Denver again was hard. The week or so I stayed and regrouped was familiar. I was among friends and acquaintances, stopping and eating at favored restaurants, not needing a GPS to find my way. Leaving was difficult, but had to happen.

As smoothly as most of the first five months had worked out, it was still work. Constant time on my phone setting up shelter on the fly, navigating, and dealing with the emotional context of the adventure was definitely harder to do on the fly than I anticipated at the start. Part of me wanted to keep one foot back in the door, so to speak, and abort the rest of the Tour. But the lease on my home still had seven more months to run, I had people along the way expecting me, and stopping now would have left me with a terrible loss of confidence in myself, having left a job undone. So I went.

My first stop was Salt Lake City, Utah, and another night with Joe Housley, one of my FB friends, and his wife. They had graciously hosted me the year before on my trip through snowy Utah. It was nice to visit and catch up with them. I also had time to look up another of my former shipmates, Jerry Moreland. Jerry and his first wife had lived in Maryland, adjacent to Washington DC, and I had stayed with them on a trip east, perhaps thirty-five years ago, and again with his current wife, Lorraine, at the time I moved to Colorado in 1996. We are the same age, and I think I look pretty good for mine, but he seemed to me to be about ten years younger that he ought to be…must be all that good clean Utah living. Jerry and Lorraine, it was a pleasure.

From SLC it was straight east through Utah and into Nevada. In Wendover I overnighted, courtesy of the local VFW post and was fortunate to leave town with additional "donations" from one of the local casinos. The next day I drove by the Bonneville Salt Flats (at street legal speed, I might add), someplace I have heard about my whole life but never quite knew where it was, made a couple stops at memorials in Carlin and Elko, Nevada before turning north into Idaho and a nights rest in Boise.

A friend of mine from Denver had moved to Boise some years ago and we still keep in touch occasionally via Facebook. Charlene was kind enough to refer me to a friend of hers who runs an interesting B&B in town and offered to host me for the night. A little off the beaten path, it reminded me of my stay in the group home on Long Island a couple months before. I had some time to consider that we are all on a path of some sort, driven to a certain beat and made to wander on a schedule not readily apparent to the next person. While I was in "here today and gone tomorrow" mode, others stayed for a week, a month, a semester or some other indeterminate length of time, to learn whatever lesson they needed to learn before moving on. I moved on.

The original plan was to head north through Cody, Wyoming, and drive through Montana and Idaho for a week or more. But the same winter weather that caused me to avoid the Dakotas also made that part of the journey impossible. I detoured through northeastern Oregon and into Washington State, arriving in Walla Walla and ending my day in the Richland/Kennewick/Pasco area with short visits to the memorials in each city.

29. *November 13, 2013*

The following day took me north and west diagonally across the state of Washington, skirting the Seattle metro area, all the way up to Sedro Woolley and the home of a cousin I hadn't seen in decades.

Stanley and I had a long and bizarre history beginning when we were both about seven or eight years old. Related by marriage, our families lived only a few miles apart and our parents were close.

One of my earliest memories of Stanley was the day our mothers took us from Los Angeles to San Diego by train for a visit to the world famous zoo there. We were nine or ten by then. Bored at hanging around with our moms all day, we begged to go down to the reptile exhibit and see their rare two-headed snake, and from there it was one adventure after another till out of nowhere we heard a woman scream, "*There they are!*" We turned to see a golf cart with my mother in it bearing down on us.

Turns out there was a major search through the entire zoo for two lost boys that day—we had no idea we were lost till she said so. I can't imagine doing that today, but sixty years ago it was just a day in the life for us.

Stanley and I stayed close until graduation from high school when we went on to our respective college experiences. I joined the Navy and he became a tank commander in the Army. We were discharged, resumed the friendship and promptly got arrested together coming back from Tijuana with some contraband (fireworks, not drugs). We got a good scare from the border patrol and were eventually released without further incident. I don't think my old VW bug ever went faster than away from that holding area. I also doubt we would get off so easily today with what amounted to nothing more than a prank.

I last saw Stanley and his family about thirty-five years ago when, on a ski trip to Whistler/Blackcomb in British Columbia, I came down to Vancouver half a day early and they came up to see me for a very nice afternoon. Of course it turned out anything but normal. My ski duffel rode down in the bus with me, and was supposed to go into baggage claim till I retrieved it later in the day, and, of course it got lost. In it was my birth certificate, clothing, ski wear, souvenirs and, oh yes, my home and car keys.

At the airport that evening, it took a while for the authorities to decide if they would let me out of Canada without identification. After landing in Los Angeles I couldn't drive home. I bummed a ride, then couldn't get into my condo...it just went on and on. This is what happens when Stanley and I get together. We found out later that the bus driver, placing my duffel apart from the others while unloading, left it just close enough to the next bus that the other driver packed it up and took it to Nanaimo on Vancouver Island. Fortunately it was returned intact a few days later.

But on this Tour I had no fear and was looking forward to seeing him. He and I have each had several "careers." His most recent was as a writer and producer of a series of award-winning documentary films. On his property is a small "shack" that he uses as his retreat while writing. It has a bed, desk, lamp, heater/stove and electricity. But it had zero plumbing requiring several treks back to the house for, well, you know. And it was November in Washington, which of course means rain, much like the other eleven months, only more so.

And of course that's where I stayed for four nights, walking a soggy pathway of dead leaves and sinister-looking mushrooms, back and forth to the house. I woke up in the middle of the night, walked out to the stoop of the shack, and peed into the leaves next to the stoop, rather than walk all the way back to the house. I'm sure he's done it a thousand times himself.

Reconnecting with a cousin I had really missed all these years was a special treat. Stanley, I know we've got at least one more adventure to come, just don't know what it will look like at the moment.

* * * * *

From his home, I drove a little way to take a ferry from Coupeville to Port Townsend, then drove out to the coast in Olympic National Park to Forks. Later in the day I had arranged to speak at an American Legion Post, Elwha Post 121, one of a handful of Native American posts in the United States. It is located on the Lower Elwha Kellam reservation just outside Port Angeles. It was close enough to Sedro Woolley that I was able to return that evening for one last night.

* * * * *

Moving south, I headed to Olympia and the memorial on the grounds of the State Capitol complex. It was wet and drizzly, and everywhere I walked it seemed moss and lichen were growing out of every pore, every gap in every walkway. I finally made it across the loamy park to the memorial and enjoyed the short visit. The Washington State Vietnam Veterans' Memorial is a distinctive wall with a silhouette of the entire map of Vietnam, north and south, cut out of the stone. Especially touching is a tribute, engraved in a prominent part of the wall, to those who came home but were never able to escape the experience. It reads:

> To all my brothers and sisters who made it back
> But never made it home.
>
> In memory
> of those who have died
> from physical and emotional wounds
> Received while serving in the Vietnam War.
> We Honor and recognize their pain and suffering.
> But above all we respect the courage
> of these Washington state residents.
>
> When our country called, you were there.
> We have not forgotten.
> You are not alone.
>
> YOU NOW REST IN GLORY
> Memorial Day, May 26, 1997

Virtually all the memorials I visited along the way honor the dead. Very few honored those who returned, only to find they never really left the experience behind.

Moving south from Olympia, I crossed the Columbia River into Oregon and knew I was heading closer to "home."

30. *November 15, 2013*

My long-time friend Gary and his wife Peggy had recently moved to Lake Oswego, just outside Portland, having lived in the Los Angeles area for most of their lives. They love it. Gary and I ran together with a pack of friends as teenagers and graduated high school together. We have stayed close ever since.

His service was spent in the army as referenced earlier in this story. I spent several days and nights with them on this trip, enjoying the company, being wined and dined by Peggy, attending a concert by a string quartet in a local brewpub, and visiting the Oregon State Vietnam Veterans' Living Memorial together, and I was grateful for the company.

The memorial is tucked into a very special corner of Washington Park, a major local destination, and so secluded that, even after climbing the steps to the stone marker for the memorial, it took a couple moments to actually understand how to access it. A long walk takes you through a short tunnel and into the Garden of Solace, a large amphitheater-like installation with massive finely manicured lawns and hedgerows.

The walk heads to the left and winds around the central core of the natural depression. It rises gently, and makes a complete circuit, so that you are crossing over the walkway from the street and continuing to make a long logarithmic spiral past large markers indicating the arc of the war.

Each marker is actually a mini-wall of broad, smooth granite representing a two-year span of the war years. The inscriptions included not only the names of the Oregon fallen from those years, but also a commentary about life in Oregon during those same years.

The trajectory of the war is seen clearly as the casualties, at the start minimal, begin to mount as the years march on. The deaths peaking, then dwindling as our political will dissipated toward the end of the conflict. A separate panel at the end of the trail honors Oregon's MIA/POWs. Then, a long and silent walk back through the same spiral. A magnificent and mournful experience; Gary, I'm so glad you were with me.

During my days with them I was also able to take side trips to see the beautiful Mid- Columbia Vietnam Veterans' Memorial in The Dalles high above and overlooking the Columbia River. There was also a smaller but extremely artistic installation in Hood River, and a memorial in Beaverton, named for an Armenian-American, Corporal Richard Janigian.

In Canby, a large installation honoring the medevac units of Vietnam, towered over the landscape with a HUEY bearing red crosses on a white field on the nose and side panels "hovering" above the ground on a sleek pedestal base. Other elements of this memorial honor American and South Vietnamese forces.

Heading south from Portland, I made brief visits to memorials in Albany and Independence. Then I turned west all the way to the coast at Newport, Oregon, where I was expecting only one memorial and was blessed with two.

One of them, a stark reminder of the war on the property of American Legion Post 116, and the other, a beautifully designed pathway along the palisade guarding the beach, with features so closely matching the natural landscape it was easy to miss one or more elements if you weren't careful.

* * * * *

I wound my way to Eugene, Oregon, home of the amazing University of Oregon Ducks football team, and my cousins Lori and Paul Reader. Lori, my youngest first cousin, and her family moved to Oregon decades ago, and, acting on an opportunity, purchased a pizza parlor and bar a block from the campus. Over the years they expanded their empire to three locations. Since my visit, they've left a daughter in charge and moved back to Southern California. Sure hope it wasn't something I said.

Back to Eugene. Lori and Paul are two family members I might see once or twice every two to three years. Our mothers, sisters in law, lived for years in the same condominium building in Encino, California. My aunt, after a long battle with cancer, passed away while I was on this journey. In the thirty years or so Lori and Paul had lived in Eugene it was my first visit to their home, and it was awesome to be there and see them.

The following day Lori took me on a tour of Eugene that included stops at the two Vietnam veterans' memorials within the city limits, one in Springfield, and stops at two of their pizza places. If you are ever in Eugene I recommend Pegasus Pizza highly, the food is great and the service extraordinary.

While there I was able to take a side trip to Bend and a visit to the Central Oregon Veterans' Memorial. This memorial park was dedicated to all US conflicts but with a very reverential piece of the park for Vietnam Veterans. On it is inscribed, from the preamble to the constitution of UNESCO:

"Since wars begin in the minds of men,
it is in the minds of men
that the defenses of peace must be constructed."

UNESCO, whatever you may think about the parent entity, does many things from the heart and soul. The quote contains a universal truth worth acknowledging, and it feels right to include it here.

Leaving family always pings the heart a bit and this was no exception. But, headed further south, I stopped at some small and wonderfully designed memorials in Sutherlin, Myrtle Creek and Grants Pass, before bedding down for the night in a borrowed RV, behind the home of another Vietnam vet in Rogue River.

The next day, after passing through Medford and visiting their memorial park, dedicated after WWI and honoring all conflicts since, I finally passed over Siskiyou Summit and coasted into California.

31. *November 24, 2013*

As might be expected due to its size and population, California is home to the greatest concentration of memorials of any state in the union. My research had uncovered nearly one hundred memorials overall, and I was determined to see them all.

Willows, a very small town north and west of Sacramento, has a commemorative Clock Tower. I struggled to find this modest memorial that turned out to be behind a strip mall. I inquired at three separate businesses in the center before someone actually knew what I was talking about. That pissed me off a little. A receptionist was kind enough to take a few moments out of her workday and guide me to the site. At the base of the clock tower's post were three small plaques dedicated to three fallen area residents. The plaques are not very prominent, but are there for people to see and take note of if they would just open their eyes and look. Neglect can be frustrating. But this wouldn't be the worst case I would see at a memorial in California.

From Willows it was a short Drive to Paradise; Paradise, California, that is, and the home of another of my shipmates from so long ago. Alan and I have had sporadic contact over the decades. Alan Kuentz was self-educated and probably the most well-read sailor in my division. He was also my first friend aboard ship. In Norfolk, there were very few west coast sailors at all, and very few I was comfortable with at first.

Alan eventually retired from the navy and worked in the shipyard in San Diego before a second retirement. Now he and his wife live a quiet, comfortable life in the country. I was there several days in late November, and enjoyed Thanksgiving dinner with his family. During that time the three of us took a day trip to Grass Valley and Nevada City, two small cities that decided to honor their fallen local heroes in a very unusual and big way.

Grass valley lost five sons in Vietnam, and Nevada City lost ten. One thing they have plenty of in both cities are overpasses along the main highways that run through their valleys. All of their local heroes have been memorialized individually on large plaques that are posted on, under or around fifteen of those bridges. Some are along the edge of the pedestrian walkways, others are mounted atop the tunnel part of the undercrossing and still others along the bulkheads or support columns. It took a while to find them all—all but one, that is. It had been removed temporarily for road reconstruction.

While in service in the late '60's, Alan and I were part of a group of sailors who had motorcycles. We rented an old run down garage for a crash pad on our off hours and toured around the state. With no plumbing and scant electricity, we had one stove and one cast iron skillet that made a lot of chili. The skillet had to be washed out with stale beer. We were living large.

During those few days I was able to make side trips to Sacramento, West Sacramento and Roseville, while striking out in Rocklin, Fair Oaks and Carmichael.

The Vietnam Veterans Memorial at the state capitol grounds is just too much for words to do it justice. It is a large installation full of plaques and other reminders; dioramas set up to give you glimpses into aspects of the veteran experience you might not otherwise appreciate: life-sized statues of soldiers at rest; one reading a letter from home; another in isolation on his cot at the Hanoi Hilton. There is a surgeon, frustrated with trying to save a mortally wounded soldier; an action scene; and more besides. Around the outside of the installation are a series of long black panels with the names of the more than 5,500 California casualties of the Vietnam War. This incredibly beautiful, emotional setting is one that should be seen by every veteran in California

* * * * *

At the end of November I cruised generally west and south to the San Francisco Bay area through Vacaville, Yountville, Rohnert park, Petaluma and San Raphael before finally crossing the Golden Gate, on my way to another cousin in Redwood City.

The memorial in Yountville is on the grounds of the Veterans' Home, a beautiful facility for our vets' last days, pristine and open. The memorial itself is as rich in beauty and emotional context as it is modest: a simple pillar, little more than waist high. Atop the pillar are two sets of hands, one set of large, strong hands giving, and two smaller, more delicate hands, receiving a folded casket flag. Holding on to one of the smaller hands is another, childlike, not wanting to let go of her mother's hand even for an instant. In Rohnert Park, on the campus of Sonoma State University, is a little park off the main entrance to the campus, with walkways and pristine lawns leading to a shaded grove. Inside the grove sits a single stone marker in memory of those Sonoma County veterans who went to Vietnam and never returned. An amazing space on a beautiful campus.

My cousin Michael and I go way back. Our family tree has forked so often that I'm not 100% sure how we are related, but I believe it. I can remember in the '70's being a very straight arrow by comparison to Michael's hippie self, even when I was TRYING to be more hip. I also remember driving twelve hours through 300 miles of heavy rain, in my old '66 VW Bug, for his wedding that lasted all of seven minutes. The wedding, that is. The marriage lasted a little longer but not much.

Our families tend to stay close. After growing up in San Carlos, he eventually settled into a home down the street in Redwood City, and this is where I stayed for nearly a week; long enough for a homemade shish-ka-bob dinner (my all time favorite), another meal out with he and his sister Kris, some time with his boys and day trips around the bay to visit memorials; one of them half the width of the state away in Sonora.

Growing up, I wasn't exactly a hawk, but I did serve. Michael was anti-war all the way. His feelings never got in the way of our friendship. But it was with mixed emotions that I took him with me to honor the memorial in Redwood City, not knowing exactly how he would react or respond. Tucked under and around the edges of a huge oak tree is a small memorial park with markers for various conflicts, including Vietnam.

Michael and I are roughly the same age; about a year apart, and I think it was clear that he knew some of the names on the marker. He grew as quiet and thoughtful as I had ever seen him. It was a good moment for both of us.

The following day I headed up to San Francisco to visit two memorials. The first was a real pain to get to. On my list it says, simply, Pier 45. In reality it is the very epicenter of tourism in San Francisco: Fisherman's Wharf. It took me more than an hour just to find a parking place, and still left a lengthy walk to the pier once I had parked.

This site is dedicated primarily to the Merchant Marine of the day and their involvement in Vietnam. A merchant ship was on display as a floating museum as well as an old diesel sub, the USS Pampanito, all decked out in flags and bunting because it was just a week ahead of Pearl Harbor Day. And the views of the bay and of Alcatraz shrouded in fog were priceless.

Later in the day I was able to reach out to an old schoolmate of mine with whom I had reconnected at my high school reunion. Susan met me at the memorial in the Presidio followed, by a dinner where we could casually catch up beyond what had been possible at the reunion. After dinner we went our separate ways and I was back at my cousin's house for a good night of rest.

Day trips around the bay brought me to some remarkable memorials in places like Berkeley, Walnut Creek, Concord, Livermore, Stockton, Hayward and two in San Jose.

The next day I flew to Los Angeles for a reunion with my immediate family and an extraordinary event.

32. *Pearl Harbor Day, 2013*

December 7th has always been a significant day in our family. It was, in 1941, the cause of my father joining the Marines and spending the arc of the War in the Pacific, only to return to San Diego, suffering from Malaria and being nursed back to health by my mother-to-be, a WAVE serving as a pharmacist's mate/nurse at the time.

December 7th also happens to be my mother's birthday. On the 5th, Michael drove me to SFO, and I caught a flight to Los Angeles for the weekend. Turns out, this December 7th would be more than just another birthday.

As I'd mentioned, my mother and sister had both been working with an organization called Operation Gratitude, one set up to send care packages to active duty military all over the world. Their mission gradually expanded to include packages that go to stateside families, veterans and first responders. Begun in humble circumstances about eight years previously, on this day they were turning out to celebrate the packaging and shipping of their one millionth package.

What my family was contributing were handmade scarves/mufflers, each about 4-6 inches wide and 4-5 feet long. My mother and sister had, by this point, completed about 250 of them, mufflers that were keeping ears and necks warm on watch stations around the world. And they were but two people enlisted in Carolyn's army of volunteers.

Carolyn is Carolyn Blashek, the founder and prime mover of Operation Gratitude. As the story goes, about eight years previous, she, a former corporate attorney, was traveling. At an airport, she happened to meet a soldier on his way back to base to report for yet another deployment to the Middle East.

After a little conversation the soldier began speaking about the futility of the mission, as he saw it. He didn't care anymore. "Why should I, when nobody else cares?" was his comment.

"I care," responded Carolyn.

"Prove it." And there it was.

She got organized. She did some research. Then she got started. At first, gathering donations and assembling boxes in her living room. Then, a miracle happened. The local Van Nuys National Guard building opened up to her and she moved into it lock, stock and donated barrel, built up the assembly line and got rolling. Eight years later, on December 7th, 2013, surrounded by thousands of well-wishers, wandering through pallet after pallet of completed packages waiting for pickup, all under a tent the size of three football fields, she celebrated the departure that day of package one million, and a good start on the second million.

For reference purposes, each box contains up to 50 different items: a book, a dvd/cd, some toiletries, a scarf/muffler, t-shirt, energy supplements; you name it, if it was small and free it went into the box. Each

> box contained $75-100 worth of goods and cost
> about $15.00 cash to mail out. Do the math and
> that comes to somewhere between $90-115,000,000
> worth of goods and cash donated in eight years,
> with the bulk of that in the last 2-3 years. Can we
> give this woman a big HOOAAAHHH?

My mother was 94 that day. Her reward for a lifetime of service to the country, her family and her friends, as well as being a supporter of Operation Gratitude, was to get to cut the cake. Standing on the podium with Carolyn's son, recently returned from his own Middle East deployment, to help with the cake, was one of her proudest moments. Nearby were local politicians, military dignitaries, actors Leah Remini and Joe Mantegna, both donors and supporters, and local television personalities. And all eyes were on mom. And she shined in her big moment.

A bit later we moseyed out to the surrounding field where a Traveling Wall had been set up for the occasion. A wonderful program followed, honoring all veterans and active military from all campaigns present, capped by a fly-by of a formation of WWII aviators in fully restored propeller-driven war birds. It was a really nice show.

Carolyn is a real mover and shaker on behalf of veterans. I was able to squeeze in only a single twenty minute interview with her during the three weeks I spent in Los Angeles, but it was a good twenty minutes.

She told me that she actually tried to enlist in her mid-40's, only to be turned down due to age. I asked her how she felt as an attorney, to be discriminated against on grounds that the government could have sued her for as a private employer, and her only response was, "No one has ever asked me that before; I'll have to think about it. I do know that I wouldn't have to carry a gun to be useful to the military. There are probably lots of jobs I could have done. The government is really wasting a valuable resource this way, don't you think?"

I couldn't agree more.

* * * * *

The rest of December passed in a blur. In addition to spending time with family and friends I hadn't seen in a very long time, I made side trips to San Diego and Orange Counties, visiting memorials in small cities like Seal Beach, Huntington Beach, Solano Beach, Mission Viejo and San Diego, and of course, the crown jewel on the naval base at Coronado.

Around the country I had hit or miss results at military bases. Some granted me instant access, others not at all. And at Norfolk, Virginia, where I had lived and worked aboard ship for 40 months, the only way to get on the base was on a tour bus with no photography permitted.

This was different. After navigating my way onto the Coronado Spit and making my way to the main gate, I was again denied entry. However, after cussing (not really) and moaning (yes, really), stating my case over and over, a base security detachment came to the gate and offered to escort me to the memorial a short distance inside the gate.

This was special. It is the U.S. Navy Vietnam Veterans' Memorial dedicated to all Naval casualties of the Vietnam War and featured not only a breathtakingly beautiful wall of remembrance, but a static display of three different types of riverine patrol craft. While my escort hovered just out of visual range, I spent some fine moments capturing the whole display on my camera. Thank you, officer, name unknown, you did me a huge favor by going above and beyond that day.

I overnighted at the home of my friends, Dick and Barbara Riegler, people I have known for well over thirty years and hadn't seen for about twenty. We had skied together and partied before their marriage. I took them to a Springsteen concert at the LA Coliseum as a wedding present, and have always enjoyed their company. They moved to Escondido a couple of decades ago and have stayed put ever since. It was good to have a chance to catch up with them and their five children.

The next morning I was back in San Diego to see the beautiful installation at the Veterans' Museum and Memorial Center. Inside and outside a large mission style building that was the former San Diego Naval Hospital Chapel at Inspiration Point in Balboa Park, the memorial is only a small part of a complex of architecturally significant buildings, and other structures, with rich historical connections to San Diego's naval heritage. Tim Smith, the Center's docent coordinator and chief volunteer, took me around the complex for a nice visit. You do great work, Tim. Look forward to seeing you next time I visit.

About three hours later I was back with family in the San Fernando Valley and prepping for another couple of days on the road heading north.

33. *December 27, 2013*

The drive to Fresno was full of expectation. I would visit several memorials and spend time with even more family; more cousins that I keep up with but seldom get to see. There would be some spirited backgammon with my other cousin Michael, and dinner with cousin Debbie and her husband Bob McLaughlin. Bob is also a Vietnam vet and longtime veterans' advocate.

On the way north from Los Angeles, I made stops at memorials in Bakersfield, Tulare and Woodlake. The memorial in Woodlake was absolutely the worst experience of the entire journey.

Begun as an impressive achievement for a very small town, a touchstone for the celebration of the lives of the men it represented, and a source of solace and support for their families.

At its dedication it consisted of a stone pillar of arroyo rock supporting a brass plaque, all set on a platform of more arroyo rock cemented in a V-shape. Behind this formation is a granite marker and flagpole. The marker honors three local soldiers from the area who died in Vietnam. Flanking the converging sides of the V were two wooden benches supported by shorter columns of stones at each end.

> Arroyo rock is the rounded granite stone one finds in dry riverbeds all around the world. Through its early Spanish/Mexican heritage in Southern California, the Term Arroyo Seco refers to any number of dry streams found locally where this rock was harvested. Much of early Los Angeles was built from these stones.

What I'd found was a forgotten site. The landscaping was more "urban vacant lot" than park, the stones dirty and dusty, the brass plaque pitted and many of the raised bronze letters rotting. One bench had pieces of two by six lumber as a seat, one end of a plank broken off, much of the rest rotted and the paint peeling away. The other bench was missing entirely, with only the stumps of the two stone supports left standing.

It was a difficult place to be, knowing I was honoring these brave men in a place where their community was allowing them to be dishonored daily. But I did what I came to do and, this time, prayed for the community as well.

* * * * *

It had been so long since I had seen cousin Debbie that I couldn't remember ever meeting her husband Bob, and they'd been married a very long time. After dinner we went out to the garage where I set up my camera and interviewed Bob about his experience during and since Vietnam.

Bob was drafted into the Army in 1967 and wound up in the helicopter corps as crew chief/flight engineer on a Chinook, shot down a couple times during his two tours In Country, and wounded once before coming home. Bob was candid in his comments to me, about coming home to a familiar, yet foreign landscape, to friends who couldn't understand, unable to communicate the experience to anyone who hadn't been there. About how he needed the adrenaline rushes of his recent past but couldn't get there, even with fast cars, boats and motorcycles. About his life since returning to The World:

"PTSD, I had it from day one...had it before I left Vietnam, didn't know it, didn't face it, didn't want to believe it. Don't think I even ever heard of it till well after Vietnam. It is pretty easy if you're a guy and you're a hard ass and you don't think much about it. Then one day...

"My wife and daughter were away. I was watching TV and a story came up about that little girl from the cover of *Life Magazine* who was running toward the camera on Highway 1 with her clothes all burned off. It was a story about how she was doing well in America, and while watching, I broke down. Started crying and couldn't stop. And I thought, what the hell's the matter with me?

"From that day forward I had these big emotional swings. And it's not easy to be a hard ass when you start worrying about yourself crying at the drop of a hat.

"I still didn't know what was wrong...didn't have a clue. So, many years later I still worked, was still successful. I realized that every job I had, but one, involved me being on my own. That one job, inside, working with others, I didn't do well in that environment.

"I finally met this gentleman from the bay area who happened to be in charge of the Vet Centers nationwide. We talked a while, we talked about Vietnam and he said 'Bob, you need to get to a Vet Center, and you need to get there now.'

"Once I got to a Vet Center and got some counseling I discovered PTSD is real, and I had it, but after counseling, I can now cope with it."

Debbie is his second wife. He was married during and after his time in Vietnam to a woman who put up with him for about ten years before telling him that he really scared her and she couldn't deal with it any longer.

Through years of counseling with Debbie along for the sessions, life has been good for them both. His daughters are grown with their own families and at the time of this interview, his grandson was considering becoming a Marine. I asked what he thought about that, if anything. He said:

"I've given that a lot of thought. I'm extremely proud of him in spite of my experience in the service and in combat, and when I really weigh it out, even though I have PTSD and it has affected me and my family in ways I didn't anticipate I still strongly encourage him to go in. When I think about the work ethic I learned in combat; how, in a few minutes, you learn more about yourself and your fellow man than you could learn in twenty years of life experience in the United States, I really think that time in Vietnam has enabled me to be successful and accomplish everything I set out to do."

Since he retired he has been volunteering non-stop in several ways on behalf of veterans, as a member of the American Legion and VFW with stints as a Veterans' Service Officer, among the most important positions in any Post. Unofficially, he is also helping veterans as needed. He once took a veteran and the veteran's family into his own home till he could get them other forms of assistance. To this day he writes, advocates, serves and helps wherever and whenever he can.

The next morning I met Bob in downtown Fresno to explore the reminders of Vietnam as they relate to the city. First stop was the Fresno Veterans' Museum, a large complex with exhibits from all American campaigns including Vietnam, and a warm and welcome visit with the curators of the museum, all veterans themselves.

This was followed by a stop at the Lao Hmong American War Memorial in a downtown park. The Hmong, indigenous to Laos and surrounding territory, were an important asset to our efforts in that part of the world. Many Lao Hmong have come to America and settled in the Fresno area. This was the only memorial to our Hmong allies I would find in my travels.

At the Fresno VA Hospital we were met with some resistance from the complex's security force who required me to get permission from the hospital's Public Affairs Office before I could take any photos *outside*. Security concerns more than a decade after 9/11 still effect us in ways we don't expect.

Finally, we drove to the suburb of Clovis to see two memorials. The first was a beautiful sculpture garden in front of the Clovis Veterans' Center. It featured life-sized sculptures of several service members representing all wars and all service branches, in a reverential scene before another Soldier's Cross. The second was in the atrium of the Clovis Veterans' Memorial District Offices. Clovis has less than 100,000 residents. Both installations showed an incredible commitment to our veterans by a relatively small community.

I said my goodbyes and headed back to Los Angeles for Christmas with my family, and enjoyed a few more days of R&R.

34. *January 1, 2014*

New Year's Day arrived, and with it a call for me to get back on the road once more. A couple days with my mom, a few more games of Tavloo (Armenian-style backgammon) with my uncle Jimmy and I was heading east again. If I'd known what I was heading toward and how the next few months would affect me, I might not have ever left.

The continuation of the Tour began easily enough. There were memorials to see all along the day's journey to Palm Springs, and a night under the roof of my sister Suzi and brother-in-law Ron's home. Stops in places like Azusa, Colton, Monrovia, and Rancho Cucamonga all brought me closer to the last family I would see for quite a while, but after nearly a month in one spot I was eager to get back on the road and continue the Tour.

In the Springs with Suzi and Ron it was dinner and a relaxing evening. The next day she and I took a drive around the city to see the memorials in Palm Desert (all three of them) and Coachella. I said goodbye and started the drive across the rest of the desert, all the way to Arizona with one stop in a little out of the way place known as Chiriaco Summit, site of not only a Vietnam Veterans' memorial, but also the home of the George S. Patton Museum, a sprawling tribute to that fiery WWII General.

At my high school reunion a few months back I had reconnected with my old friend Frank Clark, a classmate from 2nd grade all the way through high school, and who lived just around the corner. He lives now in Lake Havasu City and offered to host me on my way through that part of the country. I was grateful for the offer. I had never been there and it was eye-opening for me. We went on a tour of the city, including London Bridge, the marina, the local Vietnam veterans' memorial site. And we shared a great dinner together.

The next morning I had a powerful urge to continue and headed north to Bullhead City. I ended the day in Kingman, home of the absolute lowest gasoline prices in the entire country. From a high of $4.85 a gallon in Chicago to only $2.84 in Kingman is a huge swing in anyone's ledger.

The two memorials I saw that day were remarkable. In Bullhead City, in a little hidden corner of an older section of the town backing up to the Colorado River, I followed a path that took me to a spit of land entirely devoted to the Arizona Veterans' Memorial.

It was a huge area featuring a wall of names of all the state's fallen servicemen, as well as huge columns flanking a central flame honoring Arizona's Medal of Honor recipients. It was fronted by hundreds of freshly laid wreaths and flags stuck into the ground with military precision, each wreath's ribbon containing the name of a lost soul.

The Kingman memorial contained a large piece of stone with several facts about our losses in Vietnam, some of which I had known and others that were new to me:

There are three sets of fathers and sons on the Wall.
39,996 were just 22 or younger
8,283 were just 19 years old
33,103 were 18 years old
12 soldiers on the wall were 17 years old
5 soldiers on the wall were 16 years old
One soldier was 15 years old
997 soldiers were killed on their
first day in Vietnam
1,448 soldiers were killed on their
last scheduled day in Vietnam
8 women are on The Wall nursing the wounded

This memorial, a project of the Vietnam Veterans of America, Mohave County, Arizona Chapter 975, is indeed sobering. Looking back, I believe this was the day everything changed.

* * * * *

Another check-in: As I've been aging I've noticed creeping signs that I'm not what I used to be, and, while I resist as much as I can, I'm reminded on a regular basis that what I could do last week (a few years ago, actually) I can no longer do as well. I've seen and felt my personal entropy even as I've fought the urge to give it additional power over me.

When I began this journey I had only recently been discharged from physical therapy after a nasty accident. My back was holding up but my knees were a problem. While I felt perfectly comfortable and absolutely pain free behind the wheel, I now had difficulty standing and walking immediately after even a short drive. And it was getting worse, not better.

Early on, I received a post on Facebook from one of my church friends in response to a post of my own, putting into words the stress and emotional toll she imagined I was facing. I actually thought I was handling the stress level very well. After all, this was a journey down a troubled past for my entire generation, and I tried to always keep my shoulders squared and head high at every turn.

Each day I was faced with the results of violent death, of mismanagement and governmental/institutional stupidity. I witnessed the heartbreak of families and entire communities and spent time in the company of veterans who had been reliving their personal experience of war on a daily basis for nearly a half-century. But I was okay...right?

35. January 7, 2013

Kingman to Flagstaff in the Arizona high country brought me into contact with the thin air at altitude I hadn't spent much time in for months, much higher than Denver where I live. I passed through snowy drifts, the only snow I would encounter till the very last day of the Tour, and spent a troubled night in the thin air, sleeping poorly and blaming it on everything other than the truth: It was getting to me. The whole thing.

From Flagstaff, it was a short run to Sedona for lunch and then on to Phoenix for a couple of days with friends Bruce and Barbara Albert and more relief than I ever expected to find.

Anthem, where they actually live, is a northern suburb of the Phoenix metro area. Wide open and clear, it is a beautiful and still semi-wild landscape in spite of the recent development surge. Within Anthem is a unique memorial. While not Vietnam-specific, it is still architecturally significant. Made of five stepped pillars within a huge prayer circle, each with an elliptical "eye" at ascending heights, it is designed so that each year, at 11:11a.m. on November 11th, Veterans' Day, the sunlight streams downward through all five "eyes" to light up the Great Seal of the United States. It serves as a reminder of what really makes this country amazing: its veterans and their sacrifices.

The Phoenix Vietnam Veterans' Memorial, adjacent to the state capitol complex, in Wesley Bolin Memorial Park is a major contribution to the national conscience of the War. It stands as only one minder in a park that includes a host of other experiential and cultural memorials, but appears to dominate the landscape due to its size and scope.

The central core of the memorial is a waist-high circular display featuring a timeline of our military involvement in Vietnam from the end of WWII. Behind and surrounding this display are tall, black granite stones with the names of all Arizona's casualties from Vietnam. Nearby is a bronze sculpture of three soldiers, one shouldering a wounded comrade and another trying to pull the others to safety. There are many other elements to it, and the memorial was so large and complex that it was impossible to get it all in any one photograph. This was my second visit to this particular memorial and it was as satisfying as the first time.

Staying with Bruce and Barbara was a real treat. Our families have known each other for decades and through several changes in residence. These were the kind of friends you never lose track of. Great food and conversation, a comfortable bed; what else is there one could reasonable hope for?

Before I left I had told Barbara about my knee issues and she pulled out an old Nikken magnetic car seat pad to give me. It brought back memories nearly twenty years old, when I first moved to Colorado: I had been rear-ended on the freeway four times in three years (yes, I seem to be a magnet for careless drivers) and my lower back was in flames. She loaned me a pad at the time, and over the four days of travel between Los Angeles and Colorado Springs I never noticed a twinge or gave my back a moment's thought.

I gratefully accepted the gift this time, hardly expecting lightning to strike twice, but it did; the relief was almost immediate. For the first time in months I could walk up a flight of steps like a teenager instead of crab-walking one step at a time. Since there would be many flights of stairs along the way, knolls and valleys to traverse on foot, this was a good thing. Barb, I really do owe you.

Fountain Hills, another suburb of Phoenix, hosts a Vietnam Veterans' memorial with an added feature. It includes a tribute to Bob Hope, one of the greatest of entertainers and a true friend to the American GI during Vietnam, as he had been known for his annual visits to the troops.

I venture a guess that Bob Hope has been gone too long to have much of an impact on the consciousness of the modern soldier. His passing in 2003, at the age of 100, was pretty much the end of an era. Other entertainers make pilgrimages to our men and women around the world from time to time, as he did but nobody did it as well and for as long as Bob Hope. Thanks for the memories.

The path from Phoenix to Tucson through Casa Grande is one I had done three years before, and one that left me a little peeved. I had gone to Casa Grande to see the small but colorful memorial in a local city park, but somehow my notes had vanished. I went to their Parks & Recreation office for some direction only to find nobody knew where it was.

Turns out it was in a park just a few short blocks from the offices and I was a little miffed that they didn't know about something in their own backyard, but I got over it. Because it was important to me doesn't mean it should be important to everyone.

After Tucson I was done with Arizona.

* * * * *

New Mexico: Land of Enchantment; high and low elevations and long distances between destinations. But I had high expectations, having researched the state and seen photos of many of the installations I was going to visit. And while I was not disappointed with what I saw, I began feeling the fatigue setting in, day by day, mile after mile, alone on the road and tired of my own voice.

My first stop in this harsh and arid landscape was Truth or Consequences, New Mexico, the only city in the United States named after a radio show…really. This sleepy little town of just over 6,000 people is home to a very large memorial park dominated by an 80% scale replica of The Wall. Formerly one of the Traveling Walls, it was retired and purchased for use as a permanent memorial. The park also includes a giant five-pointed star sculpted into the ground, very much like the incredible figures on the ground in Nazca Peru, so large and so remote that "only the gods can see them."

There are markers at each point of the star, each place where the bases of the points meet, and places in between that provide a timeline of US military actions, from the Revolutionary War on. The site hosts a collection of other eclectic displays such as an old naval cannon next to a mini-Statue of Liberty.

The Hamilton Military Museum is part of the complex and includes several impressive artifacts of the Vietnam War, including a very respectful and prominent display on the life and death of local hero. Specialist 4th Class Thomas Williams, killed in action in Vietnam, June 20, 1969 in an action for which he was posthumously awarded the Bronze Star. The display includes a photo of his mother visiting his name on The Wall in Washington DC as well as the actual telegram notifying the family of the disposition of his remains; the first and only one I've seen.

After a forgettable dinner and a night in a fleabag motel in the heart of town, I was off the next day to Albuquerque and a Sunday visit with a very interesting gentleman.

The Reverend Jac Blackman, Senior Minister of the Albuquerque Center for Spiritual Living, offered, at the drop of a hat his very welcome hospitality. I cruised into the city and maneuvered my way through the maze of unfamiliar streets to his church, arriving about five minutes after the start of the service, and snuck in through a side door. Jac has an interesting style, something between Frederick March (for you older readers) and comedian Lewis Black. He was very skilled at holding and entertaining an audience. After the service he led me back to his home where I settled in before heading out to visit memorials in Albuquerque, Bernalillo and Tijeras.

The New Mexico Veterans' Memorial in Albuquerque is a surprisingly expansive affair, with not one, but two memorial parks, adjacent yet each separate and distinct. The larger setting includes a partially covered amphitheater for gatherings and ceremonies, while in the distance are a number of blank marble stones of varying heights and concentric circular layouts, reminiscent of Stonehenge. The other area has more traditional steles with names, dates and other information. Flanking the steles is a beautiful full-sized sculpture of a soldier back from patrol, weary, yet respectfully kneeling before his rifle positioned as a Soldier's Cross. It was perfect.

Back to Jac's. We talked for a long time before heading out for dinner at one of his favorite restaurants. We feasted on Indian cuisine, the sub-continental variety, and it was great. After a pleasant night and a good rest I was on my way. Jac has since retired and his church is in great hands with their new Senior Minister Kylie Renner and a spiritual community I hope I can revisit sometime in the near future.

That next day took me in a great circle route west and north, past Shiprock to memorials in Grants and Gallup before landing in Farmington for the night.

Farmington, in the Four Corners area of New Mexico, was the scene of one of my more curious experiences. I stopped at a fast food place for inexpensive dinner. While disposing of my trash I was approached by an elder Native American man asking for anything I might be throwing away so he could eat a bite or two. I looked at him for a second blankly, shrugging my shoulders as if to say "too late," and turned and walked away. I got to my car and sat a moment before going back and giving him two dollars so he could get a couple burgers off the value menu, and got back into my car to leave. While programming my GPS I heard a tapping on my window.

It was the same man. I rolled down the window thinking he came out to thank me. He asked "Do you have eleven more cents for the tax?" I had to laugh, and gave him eleven more cents. Then he turned away, and instead of going back inside, walked away from the restaurant. I got hustled by someone with a little experience. Had a little coyote in him, I bet. Hey, it was still my good deed for the day.

The motel in Farmington was okay but didn't give me a lot of rest. I tried, but the altitude was really kicking my butt. It was a little higher than Denver. I tossed and turned without being able to hit that sweet spot that would allow me to zonk out completely. It was a link in the chain of stress and fatigue from which I never was quite able to recover the rest of the Tour.

* * * * *

A modest drive to Taos, and a short jump over the hill to the east, brought me to the memorial at Angel Fire, New Mexico. I had previously visited this memorial nearly twenty years earlier when Dr. Victor Westphall, the creator of this incredible complex, was still alive and vital. Even then he had been reduced physically to roaming the complex in a wheelchair, but his mind was still sharp and insightful.

His son, David, was killed in Vietnam. David, by all accounts, was a gentle and loving man who wound up in a place he had no business being and paid the price, along with the rest of his family. At the time of that long ago visit I remember only the stark white chapel and the bare bones museum artifacts on display.

The complex has grown exponentially, with an outdoor arena for programs, a visitors center, a larger museum area, walking paths and more. The chapel was still the touchstone for me, rising like a huge white sail from the floor of the desert, beckoning to all to visit and learn a little more about our history.

A particularly poignant display is a sculpture by "Maddog" Herrera, of a well worn sculpted head on a plain pine pedestal with the legend "Touch me, feel my pain, anguish and hope." It has been touched many times, the scalp worn smoother by thousands of loving hands while on display over the years.

Sometime before his passing, Dr. Westphall journeyed to Vietnam. He took some soil from the site in Angel Fire, got as close as he could to the spot where his son was killed, and scattered it there. Then he brought back some dirt from Vietnam to scatter around the memorial grounds in Angel Fire.

Operated at least for a time by the Disabled American Veterans, this incredible site serves as a touchstone for veterans from all over the country and has a spot on many veterans' bucket lists.

Back west, over the hump to Taos and an evening of spiritual community at the local teaching chapter for the Centers for Spiritual Living led by my host for the evening, Alicia. She and her husband have a home high up and away from the town in a beautiful, hilly area. I didn't get to see much on arrival at night, but was a hard place to tear myself away from in the morning. It was just another one of my growing list of favorite places to live around the country.

* * * * *

From Taos in the north I headed almost due south three quarters of the way to Mexico proper, to the town of Roswell. Ironically, I did not find the memorial I was looking for in Roswell, but space aliens were everywhere. Drawings, sculptures and cheap plastic caricatures of aliens hang out near park benches and outside restaurants. In museums and other touristy attractions, the legacy of Area 51was everywhere to be seen. Spooky? Not really, just a town trying to have a little fun with a legend.

Turns out, Arizona and New Mexico were only warm-ups for what was to come. The next day began a series of hard days on the road: longer days than I had yet experienced, each one drawing down on my patience on the road, my energy and will to continue. That is what Texas can do to you.

36. *January 23, 2013*

I had not been to Texas during my life except for a couple touchdowns and plane changes in Houston, never leaving the airport. But this visit was by automobile and it would last seventeen days of grueling, mostly boring, high mileage driving day in and day out.

Day one of the Texas leg consisted of a route south and west from Roswell to El Paso, with a pit stop in Carlsbad. The memorial in Carlsbad was a distinctive mini-wall: a brilliant square piece of black polished marble with the faces of twelve hometown boys etched into the stone with some details of their short lives, most notably their dates of birth and death. All but one perished in Vietnam and the one soldier who came home only lived a few years before passing, likely, but not conclusively, from injuries sustained in the war.

From Carlsbad on, it was the most desolate piece of road I have ever traveled. I saw very little manmade anything along the way. There were no other cars on my side of the road the entire161 miles to El Paso.

Starved for both food and human presence, I happened to stop at Mae's Café in Cornudas, Texas. A big sign outside proclaimed, "Mae is Back." The rush of customers happy to see Mae must have happened before I got there as I was the only customer from the time I arrived to the moment I left. Must be hard to make a living way out there. The irony is, the burger I had was probably one of the top three burgers I've eaten in my entire life. I hope more people have found Mae by now, as those burgers need to keep coming off the line.

The memorial in downtown El Paso was small but prominent and honored not only those we lost in Vietnam but Cambodia as well. A night in a local motel and I was off the next morning for a very long drive to Del Rio, nearly 450 miles away.

I arrived exhausted, hot, tired and dirty, at the home of Murray Kachel, commander of the local American Legion Post, and a retired air traffic controller, who acted as my host for the visit. As retired military he was able to get me access to Del Rio Air Force Base, and he had lined up an interview with the base's public affairs staff for an article in an upcoming base newspaper.

Del Rio was also home to the Val Verde County Vietnam Veterans' Memorial outside the Chamber of Commerce building. Even though I had gotten an exceptionally early start in El Paso, and burned as little daylight racing south to Del Rio, it was starting to get dark as we left the Chamber building and headed for dinner. And a good night's rest.

San Angelo beckoned the next day. San Angelo is home to the Concho Valley Vietnam Veterans' Memorial, honoring the fallen from more than a dozen counties in South Central Texas. It features a an unarmed Slick mounted on a pedestal as well as other displays, each representing devotion to a subset of veterans as well as MIA/POWs. It also acts as a collection point for donations to veterans of all conflicts, thanks to the ongoing efforts of local veterans' organizations to help their own.

In Vietnam the Iriquois/Bell helicopter known more familiarly as the Huey served in many capacities and configurations. Most people are well acquainted with the Huey gunships from a score of movies about the war. Hueys were also outfitted for medevac duties, light transport and a host of other tasks. "Slicks" were simply Hueys that were weaponless and therefore more streamlined.

The following day I limped into the Permian Basin, having covered more than a thousand miles in the previous three days. I was eager for a rest with a member of the local CSL center, graciously arranged by the senior minister.

It being Sunday, I attended church with my host before retiring to their home to unpack for my stay. I set out to visit several memorials in neighboring towns. I was extremely grateful for the hospitality as the oil boom in west Texas had created a spike in the cost of hotel rooms, where they were even available, to 3-4 times their pre-boom prices.

After a visit to the memorial in Odessa I drove straight to the Permian Basin Memorial, one that I had been eagerly anticipating. Some time before, a friend from Midland who roomed with me in Denver had shown me some impressive photos but I had to see it for myself. Reality was even more spectacular.

The memorial was for those fallen representing about 30 counties in the basin. In addition to the wall of names and plaques, was a drama being played out in stop-action.

It consisted of a grouping of three life-sized bronze soldiers, two of them supporting an injured brother, one of them signaling with his rifle to an incoming Huey arriving to get them the hell out of Dodge.

But most moving of all was a boulder, upon which was mounted a simple piece of black marble, and a profound inscription:

> Not Everyone who Lost His
> Life in Vietnam Died There.
> Not Everyone who Came Home
> From Vietnam Ever Left There.

This wasn't the first time I had seen the sentiment expressed, but never as starkly simple and direct. It was/is a humbling thought, and on this journey I met all too many veterans who never quite seemed to make it all the way back.

There is a wonderful memorial park in Big Spring, Texas, that I visited the following day. Expansive and well designed, the Vietnam-era displays included not only an Apache gunship and a medevac Huey, but also an A4 Phantom jet in a posture that suggests it is just pulling out of a treetop run and heading back into the open sky. With its combat paint job, camo on top and a sky grey undercarriage, it blends into the sky from below, and merges with the ground clutter from above.

During a shipboard refueling at sea from an aircraft carrier just south of the DMZ, an air strike was called and we were able to witness the takeoffs and landings of several aircraft types from a distance of 60-70 feet to starboard of the carrier. My favorite was always the A4 Phantom, elegant at both ends of the ship. It was the most versatile and maneuverable aircraft of its day, and the mainstay of our ground and sea/air operations during the entire conflict.

37. *January 29, 2013*

My destination for that night was the home of a special couple in Lubbock. My Denver friend, Kathy, moved with her new husband, John Miller, an Air Force veteran, to his home in Texas. It was a treat to see them both so far from my own home. In fact, about four years earlier I bought my home from Kathy and her sister, who inherited it from their father, a WWII veteran, upon his passing.

John and Kathy were wonderful and enthusiastic hosts. All I ever knew about Lubbock was from that '80's song lyric by Mac Davis "Happiness is Lubbock, Texas in your rear view mirror." By the end of the song it was looking pretty good to the singer. I found the city to be expansive, energetic and historic.

My friends took me to the Lubbock Veterans' Memorial, a beautifully designed memorial park that honored our nation's veterans of all campaigns, collectively and individually, in a setting that dominated the park. Its wings opened like arms stretching to gather in all who would come and appreciate the sacrifices it honors. There are names of nearly 150 Lubbock area soldiers who perished in Vietnam alone.

John looked long and hard before finding the brick engraved with his father's name and information on it. Someday John's name will likely be on another brick in this memorial.

The memorial's face included an interesting quotation from Joseph Campbell, a man known for his studies on mythology and how it defines our reality. I've discovered how universal a truth it really is over the past year as I've been paying more attention to other people and their passions and contributions on behalf of all veterans:

A Hero is
Someone who
Has given his
Or her life to
Something bigger than
Oneself

After the visit to the memorial we traveled a little north of town to the Silent Wings Museum. It houses a collection of WWII memorabilia devoted to gliders used in combat, especially in the European theater. The gliders have been highlighted in films such as *The Longest Day*, *A Bridge Too Far* and *Saving Private Ryan*. But I understood their radical nature, their frailty and their crucial mission. The reality was something else.

It was hard to believe that people actually went up in these contraptions and came down again safely. It was downright scary to think about. And those brave souls who chose to pilot them were indeed part of The Greatest Generation, when it came time to do something difficult; something about which your mother would definitely not approve. My hat is off to all those who did this particular duty, and I recommend visiting this museum if and when you choose to visit Lubbock. It was an amazing and unique experience. Thank you, John and Kathy.

A little drive north and east brought me back into South-ern Oklahoma for brief stops in Lawton and Hugo and visits to each city's Vietnam veterans' memorials.

*   *   *   *   *

For the last week or so a few subtle but worrying signs were pop-ping up in my consciousness that I kept pushing back. Things were coming to a head for me internally and I spent a fitful night in a local motel before starting out again the next morn-ing for Dallas, hardly refreshed but determined to continue.

A drive due south to Canton became a 108.4 mile chal-lenge. It was by far the shortest day trip during my Texas visit, and one of the most difficult. I had a headache, a little vertigo and tightness in my scalp. There was nothing I could point to as the cause, but concentration became a struggle.

Fortunately, the docent at the museum attached to the me-morial in Canton gave me a lot of space to relax, hydrate and pull it together. I've learned that those who choose to cater to visiting veterans get to see it all laid out in front of them, and through training or experience, can recognize a person on the edge. I wasn't yet ready to admit to being that much in need…I could handle it. But he knew better and knew just how to help a guy get past it with some dignity.

After a rest at the museum I toured the amazing memorial. They had pulled off some incredible exhibits. There is a Marine Slick on a pedestal swooping in for a recovery, a huge Danforth anchor off a sizable Navy ship of the line, and an Air Force Phantom aircraft so low to the ground and accessible that I reached out and touched its tail assembly. It was thrilling to be so up close and personal with it.

Oddly, there was also a small Coast Guard Cutter, the Sabi-ne Pass, permanently housed, literally, in a hole in the ground. Ground cover and gravel snug to the waterline was designed to make it look as if it was cruising over the grass.

I was soon back in the car and on the road west to Kaufman, and a stop at its memorial park. The park included an 80% reproduction of The Wall, among other exhibits. I took the photos automatically, hardly appreciating what I was seeing.

On to Dallas proper. I had been looking forward to this visit and a reunion of sorts with my old friend Vicki, the ex-wife of my best friend Preston, who had passed away a couple of years before. I was eagerly anticipating about thirty years of catching up. Instead, on the outskirts of the city, I saw the Dallas VA hospital. Something clicked and, without hesitation, I pulled in and checked into the ER.

After several hours of examination and observation, they couldn't find anything wrong, in spite of what I told them I was doing and experiencing. A couple of prescriptions (for what I don't even remember) and I was on my way to see Vicki. We had a nice visit, I saw a few things around Dallas, and in spite of the ice storm and freezing rain that swept over the city, spent an enjoyable Sunday morning at the CSL Dallas center.

> My visit to Dallas was at the very end of month eight. I was at a very low point, emotionally and physically. I called my friend Polly Letofsky, the brave and hardy soul who walked around the world. I asked her just how she was able to keep her spirits up and keep going. She replied, "I cried a lot, and every couple of months I needed to stay in one place for about a week or so to recharge. Just pace yourself." Like so much of life, this was easier said than done. Yet I am so grateful for her support of my journey.

38. February 2, 2013

The ice storm that struck that region of Texas caused a slight interruption in my schedule. I had planned to head west to Ranger and Mineral Wells, but my contact in Mineral Wells warned me against coming due to terrible road conditions in that part of the state. The extra day I was able to spend in Dallas was a godsend: a free day to do anything or nothing, which is pretty much what I did.

Next up was Waco. I grew up having negative connotations about Waco for a host of reasons, not the least of which was the story of David Koresh, the Branch Davidians and the horror that resulted.

That preconception couldn't have been more alien to my experience. Waco was a beautiful city, and the McLennan County Vietnam Veterans' Memorial, right on the banks of the Brazos River, does credit to the city. It was a cold and grey day there in early February, but the emotional context of the memorial left me feeling warm and welcomed at this hallowed site. While driving through the city I stumbled across a fine memorial park devoted to 9/11, one of several I would see along the way.

A side trip to Burnet rejuvenated me in ways I can barely form into thoughts. My old shipmate, Joe Fischer, had long since retired and he and Barbara had moved from Kentucky to the ruggedly beautiful Texas Hill Country. I spent an evening in their home for a night of catching up and recounting old stories…the time we snuck two women aboard ship in Buenos Aires and took them into the engine room for a little adult fun(we hoped), until one of them stuck her foot into an open bucket of paint and screamed loud enough to bring the watch captain down on us…the time on the national mall in D.C. when we were so drunk we played football with a "newly" empty bottle of Cutty Sark. Amazing we didn't kill each other.

There was more, but we didn't want to chase Barbara out of the room, so we kept it reasonably clean. I explained to her how ironic it was that even though my lowest score on the Basic Battery Test upon enlisting was in mechanical aptitude, the navy was hell bent on make me a machinists mate; probably the worst MM in the history of the Navy. Joe's response: "Yeah, it was funny to watch."

I left them unwillingly. It was one of the best experiences I would have the rest of the way. But I had to go.

On to Austin and another reconnection to an old high school classmate, Dan Komer, who offered up his home to me for the night. I hadn't seen Dan for the full fifty years since graduation when he appeared at the reunion to everyone's surprise. Thank you, Dan, for taking me in and giving me a little support.

The Texas State Cemetery in Austin not only houses the city's Vietnam Veterans' Memorial, but also the gravesite of Stephen F. Austin. He is widely regarded as the Father of Texas, a powerful figure at the time of the battle for the Alamo in San Antonio, my next day's destination.

> While in Dallas I was able to see a scaled-down version of the new Texas State Vietnam Veterans' Memorial in the aviation museum of the Addison Airport. The memorial was scheduled to be unveiled near the State Capitol building in Austin just a month after my visit. An action scene, the sculpture portrays a squad of soldiers on alert in the boonies, vigilant and ready, with a radioman reporting in their situation. Placed inside the large base of the memorial will be replica dog tags from each of the more than 3,400 Texans who died in Vietnam.

Working my way through old San Antonio, I had time to kill before meeting up with my contact Alejandro Sifuentes. He was a member of my greater church community and a locally renowned artist and silversmith. After nearly a half hour of looking for a parking space near the Alamo I finally walked around the area and spotted the cultural landmark. Once it dominated all the open space around it. Now, squeezed into a little slot between larger structures, the Alamo is invisible until you are virtually in front of the mission itself, sitting directly across from the Crockett Hotel.

There is a beautiful marble installation adjacent to the Alamo with life-sized statues of Davy Crockett, Colonel Travis, Jim Bowie and other defenders of the site, along with the engraved names of all the defenders of record.

Alejandro's studio is located in La Villita, the historic art district of San Antonio. It looks very much like Olvera Street in Los Angeles, except more authentic. I arrived at the appointed hour and, after getting comfortable with each other and giving Alejandro time to clean up a few details at the studio, we walked together roughly 8-9 blocks to the site of the Vietnam Veterans' Memorial outside the San Antonio Municipal Auditorium. This memorial is remarkable on several counts.

The artist and sculptor, Austin Deuel, served in Vietnam. The memorial, double life-sized, is his recollection of a scene from the battle for Hill 881 South, April 30, 1967, a battle largely forgotten except for the families and friends of the fifty U.S. Marines and 250 South Vietnamese Regular Army who died there. It features a Marine kneeling over the body of a wounded brother-in-arms and yelling for a medic on a patch of bare, uneven ground.

Concealed inside the memorial is a list of the names, serial numbers, branches and dates of service of the more than 60,000 men and women from the San Antonio area who served In Country.

The wounded soldier's helmet is shown upturned and off to the edge of the memorial. From time to time, people passing by will put flowers in the hat as a symbol of peace, love and thanks for our veterans' collective sacrifice.

> I had unknowingly been seeing Austin Deuel's work in several cities around the country, notably the Patton memorial in California and the Women's memorial in Phoenix, AZ. This ex-Marine and prolific artist has excelled in presenting the military experience in an extraordinarily heartfelt and graphic way.

Later, over dinner and drinks, I was able to hear Alejandro's story and bond a little with a very kind soul. After a night in a friend's borrowed home, I was on my way south through to

McAllen, near the very foot of the state, on the Rio Grande near Rio Bravo, Mexico.

* * * * *

The ride south was about 275 miles of desert and more desert broken up by the occasional small town. I took a pit stop in Alice, Texas, and visited their Vietnam Veterans' Memorial. I paid my respects before heading even farther south.

The McAllen memorial was a pretty amazing site: an expansive plaza surrounded by absolutely nothing, with a tall black marble spire at the center reaching for the heavens, perhaps fort to fifty feet in height, surrounded by bricked paths entering the plaza from multiple directions, and circling the spire at a respectful distance.

Off to the side is a memorial garden of large, polished black marble slabs, with displays honoring Texas' Medal of Honor recipients over the decades.

The site commemorated campaigns, as well as details of the sacrifices of Texas' sons and daughters during the entire 20th century. An unusual aspect of the memorial is its start date for the war in Vietnam. It gives a beginning in 1954, much earlier than any other memorial I have seen, and guided me to do a little research.

Along the way, different memorials have indicated different spans of time for the Vietnam War. Most give the starting date as 1961, but some place the start as early as 1959 and as late as 1964. I looked into why. The fact is, Americans had been in Southeast Asia since the end of WWII, and aided France during the First Indo-China War from 1946 to the fall of Dien Bien Phu in 1954. American military advisors were In Country as early as 1951-52. With the rout of the French forces, our advisors began assisting the South Vietnamese Army in 1955. Our advisor levels tripled in 1961, and following the Gulf of Tonkin incident in 1964, our first "dedicated" combat troops arrived in 1965. And the rest, as they say, is history, leading up to the fall of Saigon on April 30, 1975, and the end of our military involvement.

After more than three thousand miles of driving through the state over seventeen days, I found myself a little bit east to Harlingen, hanging a big left turn and heading gradually up and out of Texas along the Gulf Coast.

Religious references are common along this stretch of American coast: Padre Island, South Padre Island, Corpus Christi, Blessing, etc. These were not so subtle reminders of what I was doing on this trip, what I was hoping to accomplish with my own spiritual pathway. Was I succeeding? Was I making a difference? I believed so. I still believe it.

I haven't mentioned it before now, but the story wouldn't be complete without referencing a pivotal comment in another movie, *What the Bleep Do We Know*, a film released in 2004 that set the New Thought movement buzzing…what is basically a layman's look at quantum physics set loosely around a fictional scenario, including commentary from a group of *very* smart people. It is a film I saw over and over again, gaining more appreciation for it with each viewing.

One of the commentators was David Albert, PhD. At the time he was a professor and the director of the Philosophical Foundations of Physics at Columbia University. He was not my favorite interview in the movie, due to some nervous personal mannerisms and I found him difficult to watch. I was in the habit of tuning him out until one viewing when what I heard rocked me to my core. He said, "It's a puzzle why we should think something like, by acting now we can affect the future but not the past."

This one statement became key to my journey: how can I use what I have learned, and whatever skills I may possess, to help those most directly affected by our experience of Vietnam, the families and friends of the fallen, and even those who fell in battle themselves? Not only those who came back, but those who didn't.

I feel very strongly that any prayer I might offer has the possibility, the likelihood even, of reframing the past, of easing the psychic burden, of increasing understanding of events and our world. Otherwise, why do it?

This is why I pray over each memorial site I visit: for the fallen, for the families, for the communities and for individual units. For whatever I find in the moment, whatever speaks out to me that needs attention. It is work. It is thrilling, it is necessary and it is a joy. At the same time, it is wearying to the spirit.

* * * * *

After driving all day I was late getting to Blessing. Lunch in Corpus Christi and a visit to the Vietnam Veterans' Memorial in Yorktown were the highlights of a very long day encompassing nearly 400 miles.

I got an interesting welcome in Blessing. I met my contact at the American Legion Post, not hard to find as it was the only thing generating any traffic in this little town. The post was also the best restaurant in town.

After sharing a couple of beers with the officers of the post and having a surprisingly good dinner, they directed my tired body to the Blessing Hotel, courtesy of a reservation they made in anticipation of my visit. Perhaps the oldest hotel I stayed in during the entire Tour, it was well over 100 years of age. I got the room key at the Post, which was a good thing because there wasn't a soul at the hotel. I was virtually the only one there. It took a while to find my room.

It happened to be a freakishly cold night in early February and the room was totally unheated, with unnaturally high ceilings. I did manage to find two small space heaters that helped, but the warm air went so high up so quickly that it took a very long time to warm the room.

It was apparent the hotel had not experienced any recent renovation. The plumbing in the bathroom was installed sometime in the early 20th century for guests that must have been about a foot shorter than I; this was all very quaint and interesting, but I'm glad I was only there for one night.

The next morning it was a very short trip to Bay City and a visit to the memorial in front of the Matagorda County Courthouse, before heading back to the coast and the scenic route to Galveston. The memorial in Galveston commemorates the seventy-five residents of Galveston County who were KIA during those turbulent times, and also honored a seventy-sixth casualty, Charles J. Sabatier, who died after the completion of the memorial. The citation reads:

"In 1968 during the first Tet Offensive, Charlie was pinned down in heavy crossfire, when he heard the call of another soldier in need. Running across the swampy battlefield to help, he felt a bullet enter his back. Charlie spent the rest of his life in a wheelchair, but spent his career with his wife Peggy working for the dignity of people with disabilities. A true American patriot, distinguished lawyer, and national advocate for the disabled, Charles Sabatier died in 2009 directly, if not immediately, from his combat injuries. Welcome home at long last, Brother."

Thank you, Charles, for being there. The world needs many more like you.

Up the road a bit from Galveston is Houston, home to the only memorial I saw completely devoted to the people of South Vietnam, the freedom-loving citizens, civilian employees and soldiers who fought to stave off the eventual communist victory. The plaque includes a thank you for all Americans who also fought for them. The sculptures of the Vietnamese civilians, walking a country road, all their provisions and possessions stuffed onto bags thrown over their shoulders, speak volumes about the suffering and uncertainty that they endured as well.

I spent a quiet Saturday night in the home of the musical director of the Houston Center for Spiritual Living, before heading north and east and out of Texas for the first time in what seemed like forever.

39. *February 10, 2014*

Entering Louisiana from the southwest or "Heel" of the state, I headed to Lake Charles, birthplace of my former shipmate, Alan Kuentz.

Veterans' Memorial Park in Lake Charles honors Medal of Honor recipient Douglas B. Fournet, First Lieutenant, USMC, and has another exhibit special to me, a Huey that was certified as one that participated in the battle of the Ia Drang Valley, the second such reference to that pivotal battle I had come across.

Earlier in this work I made reference to the memorial devoted to Gordon Young of Drake's Branch, VA, who was KIA in the battle of Ia Drang. The battle was both a big win for the United States and an unmitigated disaster. In the aftermath both sides claimed victory. While casualty counts differ depending on which side you were listening to, we lost about 250 Marines KIA, at least as many wounded, and about 3500 enemy dead. In one fell

> *swoop, this battle convinced both Sec. McNamara that we couldn't win a war of attrition, and Ho Chi Minh that he could wait us out no matter the cost. McNamara admitted this during his testimony in the libel suit of Westmoreland v. CBS.*
>
> *Before Ia Drang the US had experienced about 1000 combat deaths. After Ia Drang, knowing in his heart that it was a lost cause, McNamara and the other powers that be, sent enough of our men and women over there that we lost another 57,000 plus over the next 10 futile years.*

A long drive up the western border of Louisiana took me to Bossier City, just outside Shreveport, and a clash with base security at Barksdale AFB. I could not get onto that base no matter what. Rather than get myself arrested, I settled for finding the memorial just inside the chain link fence surrounding the base, and snapped a couple of pictures. They were too far away for any detail, just a couple of big marble blocks in the foreground with a couple B-1 bombers in the distance.

I crossed into Arkansas and the start of a big loop that would take me back through Louisiana with stops in Fort Smith, Paris, Morrilton, Clinton and Searcy. I offered prayers to the memorials at each site. The road south took me to Little Rock and a memorial site on the grounds of the Arkansas State Capitol.

The region was in the grip of a ferocious cold snap and walking any distance outside was less than comfortable. Trudging over the brown grassy/muddy surfaces invited a lot of slipping and sliding. The sky was as uniformly grey as the stone monument I was visiting. The Arkansas State Vietnam Veterans' Memorial honored the sacrifice of the hundreds of men and women who were listed on several panels of the curved wall.

Valentine's Day was only two days away as I drove through Little Rock in search of my motel. I found an interesting billboard alongside the road. It advertised: "Buy her a diamond and get a shotgun." Something for everyone, I thought.

The next morning I awoke to the same icy conditions; just a trickle of really fine ice pellets falling everywhere, enough to make the roads really tricky, and a drive of any length interminable. I had 319 miles to push through that day, all the way to Ville Platte, Louisiana. I was able to go as fast as 35 miles per hour in some spots along the slippery highway, (sometimes as little as 15 MPH), all the way to Ruston, roughly 170 miles, and wondered, with my eyes hurting and leg muscles cramping, if I was going to make it another 150 miles. Then a miracle happened.

At the south edge of Ruston, the state police were closing the road I had just traveled to northbound traffic, and looking south, the road was completely clear of ice. A little damp, perhaps, but nothing to keep me under the posted speed limit the rest of the way.

Ville Platte was serious Cajun country, looking very much like the landscape I remember from the movie *Deliverance*, but friendlier, and with better food. I don't even remember if the restaurant where I had dinner had a sign, but it was the very best Cajun cooking I had ever experienced.

* * * * *

I woke up reasonably refreshed and ready to face a long day of travel and exploration. There were nine memorials to see in seven cities stretching nearly 300 miles across lower Louisiana.

The memorial park in Ville Platte was a little sparse but did honor their dead from every U.S. campaign. Vietnam was represented by another Huey and a respectful stone stele with the names of the dozen men from Evangeline Parish who never made it home.

A little closer to the Gulf of Mexico, In La Fayette, were two memorials: a small one directly outside the Cajundome honoring a local Medal of Honor recipient whose citation for his efforts, cast in bronze, was truly inspirational. Captain Steven Logan Bennett is one of the few Air Force pilots to receive the MOH, deservedly so.

It had been several months since I had seen the Mississippi River on this journey, but a visit to Baton Rouge took me right back. This was easily the best day, weather-wise, of the last couple of weeks. The port and its memorial plaza were a fantastic site.

The Vietnam Experience was expressed in multiple displays and fountains. An A-7 Corsair jet aircraft, the only one of its kind I would see, sat fully armed, and looked particularly hostile on a pedestal high above the ground, in front of the wall commemorating the area's lost souls.

The day continued with stops to visit memorials in Houma and, finally, New Orleans. Houma, in Terrebonne Parish, has to be about as far away from anything as just about anywhere in the United States, right on the edge of the swamps that separate it from the Gulf, about forty miles off the beaten path. I found the memorial in Houma to be outsized for the area, a symbol of pride and sacrifice for the region that made the drive well worth it.

I had been looking forward to New Orleans for quite some time. I had last been there about ten years earlier with a girlfriend, and enjoyed the visit more than I enjoyed the girlfriend, truth be told. Where else can you get your fortune told in the rear of a Voodoo shop, head into the wild on an airboat and pet a 10 foot alligator after luring it out of hiding with marshmallows?

This time around I was looking forward to a visit with my friend Stephanie, a Louisiana native who relocated to Denver after Hurricane Katrina, and just happened to be in town for a visit. Stephanie's charming friend, Anne, offered up a spare room for the night and was wonderful company as well.

Parking near the Superdome in the heart of New Orleans was complicated, as thousands of fans were in the city for the annual NBA All-Star Game and related activities. But, I got lucky and found a spot pretty close to the stadium. The memorial was on the plaza level, one story up from the street and invisible to the public speeding by. It was an impressive tableau, featuring, among other exhibits, life-sized bronzes of three soldiers, alert for trouble as they carried a fourth injured soldier to safety.

A few blocks away on the Esplanade is a spire erected in support of the American, Vietnamese and Allied forces who served during the war. Then it was on to an incredible memorial park in Mississippi.

* * * * *

Ocean Springs, Mississippi, is home to the Mississippi Vietnam Veterans' Memorial. It is contained in a large park with some references to other campaigns, but dominated by a very different and distinct homage to the 600 plus Mississippians either KIA or MIA during the Vietnam War.

Other memorials have one or more photos engraved into their surfaces, but seldom more than a dozen. This memorial includes laser engraved photographs of each and every soldier whose name appears on the two stone walls. Coming face to face, as it were, with so many of the fallen was an incredibly emotional experience for me. It was also the only memorial I saw that flew the flags of all the Allied nations that assisted our efforts in Vietnam: Australia, New Zealand, South Korea and Thailand.

That would complete my time in Mississippi: one and done. I'm sure there are more Vietnam-specific memorials in the state, but I hadn't turned up any in my research. Alabama beckoned.

40. *February 18, 2014*

About 50 miles down the road lay Mobile, Alabama, and its massive Battleship Park. Situated at the top of Mobile Bay, it is dominated by the massive warship named after the state.

The entire park is devoted to military memorabilia of all kinds with an expansive tableau dedicated to the Vietnam veterans of two southern Alabama counties, and includes the names of all their fallen sons.

Freestanding on the ground between the two large stone panels of the memorial is a bronze statue of an older man, a father figure. Standing there, he is frozen in place, taking in all of the emotional roller coaster that accompanies a visit to any remembrance of a fallen son. In one hand he clutches a real American flag while the other holds the dried and dead remains of a floral arrangement. Engraved in the stone are a few lines written by an anonymous Vietnam vet that reads:

Vietnam-War/pain/Sorrow/Mystery/ Jungle/Swamp/Mountains/Hot
Vietnam means something—Different but the same—to all of us
Vietnam has a lasting effect of one sort or another on all Americans
Vietnam can only be understood by those of us who were there—
--and WE don't understand it

I headed south and east from Mobile to my next destination, Pensacola, Florida. I would return to Alabama in a couple days, but the Panhandle was calling out to me.

Escorted by my new friend and host Dan Kirkpatrick, I surveyed the site that included a helicopter gunship. But the most striking feature of all was a small bronze sculpture of a child, perhaps four or five years of age. She was a symbolic daughter of a returning soldier, dressed in overalls and clutching a favorite doll while wearing a combat helmet. The work is titled "Homecoming" and shows the strain of a family left behind. There is desire, fear and uncertainty in the eyes of the child, welcoming back a father who she barely remembers. It was incredibly touching and a reminder that those who remain home also serve.

Hurlburt Field, an Air Force base near Ocean City, Florida, is home to a memorial to the Forward Air Controllers. Incredibly brave men who flew low-level missions in Vietnam in airplanes that few would have ever dreamed of flying in combat: Cessnas. The role of the FAC was dramatized in 1988 in the movie *Bat 21*. Their mission profiles were many and varied, but all flew too low and too slow, virtually unarmed, and were easy targets for the enemy on the ground.

Initially denied permission to enter the base, I eventually convinced the MPs to assign me an escort for the brief time I would be there. I could see the entire memorial at a distance from outside the gate, too far away to photograph adequately, and had been really P O'd that security concerns were keeping me from going the 500 or so feet to the memorial after nearly 40,000 miles of continuous travel. The base policeman who wound up escorting me was a very nice young man who had no idea the memorial was even there or what it honored. I guess all of the past is someone's past, but not everyone's. Still ticked me off.

I drove north from Ocean City and back into Alabama, on a leg of the tour that would take me all the way up into Tennessee and Kentucky before heading back to Florida. I swear I wasn't drunk when I created my itinerary, but you wouldn't know by looking at my map.

Daleville, Alabama, is home to Fort Rucker and the US Army Aviation Museum. The museum was closed the day I was there, but the grounds outside the museum are full of tributes to various aviation units who served in Southeast Asia, including one stone honoring the Royal Australian Navy, for sending their Experimental Military Unit to serve with our helicopter assault forces from 1967-71. The Aussie's motto was short and to the point: "Get the bloody job done."

All the way up the central spine of the state took me to memorials in Prattville, Wetumpka, Clanton, Oneonta, Gadsden and Decatur before detouring west for some blues and barbeque in Memphis, Tennessee.

41. February 20, 2014

Memphis is a beautiful old town; picturesque and historic, and home to three Vietnam veterans' memorials. At the Leftwich Tennis Center, named for local hero William G. Leftwich, Jr., the memorial consisted of a black granite stone bearing a bronze bust of the Marine Lt. Colonel along with the story of his death. The rescue helicopter he was aboard crashed, along with the soldiers they had just rescued from enemy territory, into a mountainside. Among the distinctions he had earned during his service were the Navy Cross, the Air Medal, the Silver Star, the Legion of Merit and three Purple Hearts. To say he left it all on the field would be an understatement. I left him with a salute and a prayer.

Off to see memorials in Dyersburg and Clarksville, I eagerly anticipated seeing whatever might present itself the next day in Fort Campbell, Kentucky, and I wasn't disappointed. As modern military practices go, it was relatively easy to get on the base, and I was directed to the memorial park on the base adjacent to their military museum. A full complement of helicopters graced the park, including the only Loach, that I would see along the way.

The park also included a Wall of Honor to those KIA in Vietnam who also served at the base, as well as unit memorials. But the unique part of the visit was the museum. Inside were artifacts brought back from the war zone that mattered to those who called Ft. Campbell home. In addition were displays of a hooch (how they lived), C-rats (the canned and processed foods they ate), and other day-to-day reminders of the conditions in a hostile and fickle environment far, far away from everything we knew and loved. Being a "Blue Water" sailor, this was all alien to my experience in Vietnam, and can honestly say I liked it better where I was.

Meandering through Kentucky I was able to visit and pay homage to those lost and those who served in Madisonville, Russelville, Franklin, Scottsville and Glasgow, before arriving in Bardstown.

Not many outside of Kentucky have heard much, if anything, about Bardstown, Kentucky, but it was a one of the places along the way that helped me define this journey.

Among the first books on the Vietnam experience I read was the moving story of *The Sons of Bardstown* by Jim Wilson, first published in 1994. It is the story of a National Guard unit, 105 men from this small town of about 6,000, who went to Vietnam as a unit, served together at Firebase Tomahawk, an insignificant and largely forgotten posting. In 1969, in one fierce nighttime battle, the unit suffered ten KIA and nearly fifty seriously wounded. The effect on the town has been felt across multiple generations. I grew up in a city of about 33,000 where everyone seemed to know everyone else. In a city of 6,000, it seems that practically everyone was *related* to everyone else. It was a bitter time for everyone in Bardstown.

For the sake of perspective, if it happened to a city such as Los Angeles with a population at the time of about 2.5 million, it would be as if LA had lost more than 4,000 of its citizens in one night. Yet Bardstown survived and memorialized their lost sons, and continues to maintain a beautiful and historic thread in our national cultural tapestry.

Another emotional visit awaited me the next day as I went back to Frankfort to revisit the Kentucky State Vietnam Veterans' Memorial. This is perhaps the most unique memorial in the country dedicated to those who served and died in Vietnam.

The memorial is laid out in the form of a sundial whose gnomon casts a very long shadow. The gnomon itself is more than 24 feet long and its tip is more than eleven feet off the ground.

Designed by Kentucky architect Helm Roberts, the memorial honors each of the 1103 KIAs from the state with his or her own individual Memorial Day. As the shadow of the gnomon sweeps slowly across the granite surface of the memorial, lengthening and receding with the seasons, The shadow falls on each name on the anniversary of the day the soldier fell in combat.

The granite base of the sundial encompasses nearly 6400 square feet and is an architectural and engineering marvel. The site also include a meditation garden adjacent to the sundial portion, as well as a wall of names situated behind the sundial in a place where no shadow will ever fall on them again. There is much more significance to the design and execution of the memorial than I can include here, but you could look it up, or, better yet, visit.

While feeling the emotional strain of two highly charged memorial visits in the span of two days, it was almost impossible to fully decompress even as I spent a pleasant evening in the home of a member of the Center for Spiritual Living in Louisville. I enjoyed attending their service the next day (I needed a little dose of spirituality) before heading to memorials in Lexington, Winchester, Paris and Mount Sterling, and ending my journey through Kentucky in Middlesboro.

42. *February 24, 2014*

It was a long day of driving and reflecting. The interior struggle I had been keeping at bay ever since Texas was bubbling to the surface. As I lay in bed in the motel on the outskirts of Middlesboro, I was overwhelmed with nausea, a headache and an incredible tension that enveloped my entire body, especially the eight or so inches between my temples.

Not knowing what else to do and not finding a VA hospital nearby, I picked up my cell phone, called the VA's 24-hour nurse hotline and spoke to a real angel of a nurse. She kept me talking while going through her triage protocol. She kept me calm and focused until finally determining that all my symptoms pointed to stress. The best thing I could do would be to take a nice, long, hot shower; especially around the head and neck, and to get the best night's sleep I could manage.

I wish I knew her name. There are a lot of competent people at the VA, doctors and nurses who treat a huge assortment of ills on a daily basis. Their routine day would stagger most outside medical professionals. But their demeanor can also be very standoffish and impersonal. It is easy to appreciate them, but hard to actually like most of them.

This nurse was different. Throughout the entire conversation, I was the most important person in the world to her—at least that was how I felt, and I believe she talked me down from a very dangerous place. She is a blessing to the VA and to all veterans who use VA facilities. While not exactly 100%, I did feel better as I began the next day's journey through eastern Tennessee to see my friends Bill and Francine Clark in Nashville.

I've known Francine for most of my adult life. We were members of a ski club in the Los Angeles area for more than twenty years, before she moved to Nashville and met and married Bill. I had only met Bill once before, and hadn't seen either of them in a decade or so. They took me in and gave me some space to relax. After the two nights I spent with them, I was almost a human being again. One evening she invited a female friend over and cooked a marvelous dinner. Ah, domesticity.

The next evening we went out to The Bluebird Café, a small club devoted to songwriters and their music. The rule is that you can't perform at the Bluebird unless you are a songwriter. I had no idea it was even a real place. It is an integral part of the television show *Nashville* and is featured in nearly every episode. I was under the impression it had been created just for the show.

In reality, the club has been there for more than thirty years, showcasing some of the best writing and performing talent around. That night we heard four exceptional singer/songwriters perform and had a wonderful time.

During my second day in Nashville, Bill and I toured the city, had lunch at a historic diner and visited the Vietnam veterans' memorial downtown. Built into the plaza level of a midtown high-rise office complex, it features a wall dedicated to the more than 1200 Tennesseans killed in Vietnam. It includes a bronze grouping of three soldiers in combat ready postures facing the wall of names.

I have to thank Francine and Bill for their incredible generosity and kindness, not only the warmth and friendship that had seemingly not lost a beat in spite of distance and time, but also for the car battery that Bill bought as a donation to the cause. It undoubtedly prevented a lot of hassle going forward. You guys saved me in a very special and timely way. I was a stronger person leaving than when I arrived.

After a few more stops in Tennessee it was time to head for Georgia, and the city with more Vietnam-specific memorials than any other in America.

43. *March 3, 2013*

At this point, early March of 2014, I had been more than nine full months on the road. I was pretty much ready for it to be over, but there was more to see and do.

Heading south I traded the Appalachians for the Blue Ridge Mountains in the blink of a border crossing, and started a busy day of memorial visits. There were two in Gainesville, and I would not stop till I got through Alpharetta, Roswell and Smyrna. I ended the day with family in Atlanta.

My second cousin, Alex and his lovely wife Jessica moved to Atlanta some years ago. Alex is a concert pianist and college music professor, and Jessica is a violist with the Atlanta Symphony Orchestra. The previous Christmas in Los Angeles I had asked them if they could provide me some support while I was in Atlanta, and they said absolutely. I was with them for four nights and enjoyed every minute of their company. We ate in and out; I toured the area and spent a little time on my own.

I was invited to a lunch meeting of the AVVBA, the Atlanta Vietnam Veterans Business Association. Early on in my planning, I attracted a new Facebook friend in Mark Walker. Mark is an Atlanta-based Vietnam Veteran, and an officer of this group that has done some amazing things for the city.

Each year for the last twenty-plus years, the AVVBA honors another area veteran who was KIA during the war, with a plaque somewhere in the city. I had hoped to visit all of them but some eluded my efforts. AVVBA raises money in various ways, does all the logistics, plans each event with music and continues their wonderful work year after year.

The luncheon was impressive on its own. I half expected to see about twenty old guys, perhaps in some olive drab or camo gear, like so many in the Legion and VFW halls I had visited. Instead, I found a room full of more than a hundred successful businessmen and women in animated discussion and enjoying the moment.

I appreciate your support, Mark. Thank you for what you do on behalf of the rest of us.

From Atlanta I more or less crisscrossed the western part of the state; west to Bowdon, east to Griffin, west to Columbus, and wound up in a beautiful, if out of the way, memorial park outside of Cordele. To get to the Georgia Vietnam Veterans' Memorial you have to slide along secondary roads that go through some very swampy and strangely beautiful country. Suddenly, there is this expansive and open memorial park in front of you that seems to go on forever.

In addition to a Grecian style memorial to the war, there is a museum that features artifacts from several campaigns including Vietnam. On this stark and chilly early March morning it was good to spend a little time inside. The day ended with me pulling into my motel in Tallahassee, Florida, about sixty miles and a major climatic shift away.

Tallahassee was a picturesque city. The Florida State Capitol was decked out in colorful striped awnings like a tropical motel in a Jimmy Buffet song, and I loved it.

The Florida Vietnam Memorial just rose out of nowhere directly across the street from the Capitol building. A huge American Flag, perhaps thirty feet tall, hung, suspended between two tall, tapering granite towers. The lower panels of each tower were inscribed with the names of the nearly 2000 Florida dead and missing from the conflict. It was sad and proud, soaring and searing all at once, its symbolism evident to all.

On the way back to the car something seemed to break in my ankle…at least that's how it felt in the moment. I was in incredible pain and unable to put much pressure on it; just one more challenge to overcome. Eventually I was able to limp back to my car and take a breather. I had no idea what caused it—no stumble or trip, no stepping sideways on a crack. One minute good, the next, well, as you get older the universe has a way of letting you know that not everything works all of the time. This was one of those times.

* * * * *

My inability to walk without pain made this a very long day. I ended up at the home of my cousin, Vikki. Vikki is family from my father's side. His siblings scattered all over the country, with his only sister relocating from Michigan to Florida. The only time I had ever seen Vikki was in the hospital in Kansas City, nearly twenty years before, when my father was in the process of transitioning from this life to the next.

I had been eagerly anticipating this little reunion, relaxing and catching up. Instead, as soon as I arrived and said my hellos, I asked her to take me to the local VA to have someone look at my ankle. What are the odds, seeing someone for the second time in a life and having both times involve hospitals?

The good news was they couldn't find anything seriously wrong and just told me to "deal with it" with the aid of some nice pain meds. We got home about 10pm and proceeded to settle in for the night.

Vikki has been one of my long time FB friends as well, and we had set this night up nearly two years previous. Recently, her mother-in-law, having some aging issues of her own, had come to live with them, and their spare bedroom was taken. I got the recliner in the living room, and still managed a decent night's sleep.

> During this journey I slept on couches, benches, floors, mobile homes, mats and recliners. I made it a point not to turn down any accommodation and was blessed that there were so many who reached out to me with support along the way.

The next morning I left with their good wishes, for a trip down and back up the length of Florida, knowing I would be back this way in a week for another stay.

Two years before, I spent a week in and around Tampa on a trial run for the Tour. I set a schedule of visits for a half-dozen memorials, three on the west coast, one in the interior, and two more on the east coast of the state.

Another of my FB friends, a female veteran, along with a couple of her friends, met me at the memorial in Tarpon Springs. Off the coast and in a park that parallels the inland waterway sits this wonderfully understated spire. It fronts a pool of seawater large enough to host several manatees, which surfaced every few moments.

On the Tour this time, after revisits to memorials in Dunedin and Bradenton, I ended the day at a trailer park in Lakeland, Florida, owned by old friends from Colorado. Radine and Jerry retired to Florida and promptly lost their collective minds. They bought two dilapidated trailer parks, which they were struggling mightily to keep afloat. They are incredibly hard workers, so I believe they'll make it just fine. But on that night, the trailer they originally thought of putting me up in still didn't have a floor, so it was another night in a recliner in the living room of their mobile home.

Old friends of our family lived just outside Tampa and offered a room to me for the following night. Needing a real bed, I accepted. I really enjoyed seeing a face from the past, meeting her husband, sharing a meal and hearing about their life on the opposite coast from where she grew up.

* * * * *

The long distances I traveled each day, coupled with the not quite perfect sleeping arrangements in which I had lately found myself, were having a profound effect on me. I noticed myself talking less, adopting a slightly downward posture while walking rather than head up and straight, and experiencing occasional tunnel vision. I really needed a break, but this late in the game, having only another eighteen days remaining, I couldn't stop long enough to catch my own breath. I wanted that finish line to appear.

44. *March 14, 2014*

I had planned to visit Miami, stay the night, then head down to Key West. I made an executive decision to abandon the keys altogether. I couldn't make myself go that extra distance and I was secretly ashamed. It was another 500 miles, I told myself, a full day there and another day back…more wear and tear. I was still hobbling slightly from the ankle injury, tired and sore, and just looked north. I couldn't get my head turned around, so I never got to the memorial in Key West—but I will… someday.

I spent that next day in Miami, not doing much but resting and managing to fit in a lunch in Fort Lauderdale with my friend and webmaster, Tamara; she had moved back to Florida from Illinois a short time before. It didn't go well. She was energized and full of ideas for me, and I was a bump on a log. I did not hold up my end of the conversation, and when I did speak, I was usually off topic or incomplete. Sixteen days left.

* * * * *

A run up the east coast the following day brought me to and through Port St. Lucie, Sebastian and a memorable stop in Vero Beach. This was always a dream destination for me as a young man: the spring training facility for my beloved LA Dodgers. While this visit was during spring training for the upcoming 2014 baseball season, the Dodgers had long ago abandoned Florida for Arizona.

The memorial, however, was amazing. Situated on its very own island, the Veterans' Memorial Island Sanctuary, the short, thick pentagonal stone marker sits on a concrete pad next to the Intracoastal Waterway, in one of the most breathtakingly beautiful vistas I have ever seen.

Past Melbourne, and the memorial erected outside the Disabled American Veterans Post, I headed north to find some lodging for the night and wound up in Titusville along the Space Coast. In addition to the Vietnam Veterans' Memorial, Titusville also has an incredible memorial to the original Mercury Seven astronauts.

After a modest drive up the coast to the memorial in DeLand the next morning, it was full steam ahead to Gainesville and another night on my cousin's recliner. Fourteen days to go.

> I don't mean to sound unappreciative in the least for any accommodation I was given during the entire Tour. Plans often changed after a period of time. I remember that first day on the road nearly 10 months before, on the phone with my host, letting him know I was on the way, while he was on vacation, completely forgetting I was coming. People move in and out of homes, emergencies arise and it can't be helped. At least I wasn't sleeping in my

car. Often I was given more than I had any reason to expect. I may never experience such giving, such joy and uncertainty again in this life, but this year-long demonstration of love and acceptance of what is possible will be with me forever.

The next morning took me to Lake City, my final stop in Florida. A left turn in Jacksonville and I was in Georgia once again.

The Glynn County Courthouse in Brunswick was host to their Vietnam veterans' memorial set against a backdrop of old oak, palm, willow and magnolia trees dripping with moss. They formed an incredible tableau. Glynn County's fallen are honored in a beautiful setting.

Motoring through Savannah, I found the city's memorial on one of the busier esplanades in the city. It sits in a park favored by hikers, joggers, power walkers, business people out for a lunch in the sun and more. Within a pond was the map of North and South Vietnam carved into the top of a very large granite boulder. The walkways nearest the pond contain bricks engraved to honor the sacrifices and heroism of individual servicemen and servicewomen.

My day ended in Augusta. I couldn't resist taking a peek at the most famous golf course in the country. When I have watched the Masters' Tournament on television, I got a feeling for the countryside around it, how isolated and alone it must be off in the beautiful Georgia countryside.

Not so much. I found the golf course perched at the edge of a small city with crumbling infrastructure and lots of damage still visible from recent winter storms. What I could see of the golf course, around the edges of the high, white, impenetrable fencing that surrounds it from the rest of the city, was pristine and lovely to see through a bit of morning fog.

Security stopped me cold at the gate and wouldn't allow any photos taken on the grounds. I had to stand outside the gate and hope for the best. Oh well, I never expected Hootie (or whoever is now in charge) to come out and offer me a chance to play a round with them.

Somewhat refreshed after a night spent on a bed wrapped in plastic (under the sheet), I headed farther north for a visit to Hartwell, Georgia, and into South Carolina. A few days spent in coastal Carolina that lifted my spirits somewhat. As states go, South Carolina is perhaps the most beautiful, in my experience, outside California. Only eleven more days to go.

* * * * *

The drive through Anderson and Laurens to Columbia was magnificent. I arrived at Memorial Park in downtown Columbia on a beautiful day, one of only a handful without rain during the month of March. Among several other displays in this park were tributes to other campaigns, including a unique monument to the men of the China/Burma/India theater in WWII—a very important part of our war in the Pacific, and an experience that just seems lost in the mists of time.

Due south from Columbia was Boot Camp all over again. Perris Island, South Carolina, is a place that most marines think of with a hollow feeling. Marines began their basic training (boot camp) at either the Marine Corp Recruit Depot in San Diego, or here in Perris Island. I imagine the humidity factor in the summer in South Carolina can be daunting. But the drive around the base on this cool March morning was fantastic. It is among the best-maintained and most beautiful military installations I was privileged to visit. But the real treat for me in South Carolina was waiting just a few miles up the road.

I called my friend Jim Ewen in New Jersey and told him where I was. He said he started sweating just thinking about Perris Island and his own experience as a boot Marine.

Patriot's Point, along the coast just outside of Charleston, is an impressive installation of past military might and heroism. Several ships are moored and open for exploration including the USS Yorktown, a massive aircraft carrier, and the destroyer USS Laffey, both of which served with distinction in WWII.

The Laffey, in particular, gives a glimpse into the intense action during the Pacific War. Attacked by more than 20 kamikaze aircraft near the end of the war, the Laffey was struck by five suicide planes and three bombs in one attack, killing or injuring a third of her crew. The captain kept maneuvering wildly throughout the battle and was able to bring her safely to port. The Laffey served another thirty years before being decommissioned in 1975 and was put on permanent display in 1981.

But the most amazing and unanticipated display at Patriot's Point was a full-scale reproduction of a US Naval Support Base seemingly transported whole from In Country.

Authentically reproduced down to the OD paint on the buildings and corrugated roofs, to the dirt-filled fifty-five gallon drums lining the perimeter, the sandbagged gun emplacements and underground hooches, I couldn't take my eyes off of it.

Empty watchtowers reach into the sky. Silent helicopters dot the grounds inside the concertina wire. Quick glances into the hastily constructed mess hall and first aid hut give testimony to the spartan conditions our boys and girls lived in and served under. It was breathtaking.

After lunch in Charleston and quick stops at memorials in Sumter and Conway, I was on my way to the last state in the tour, North Carolina. There were still some wonderful new friends to meet in these last days. But funds had become a challenge and my spirits rose and fell daily, sometimes hourly. And the will to continue flagged from time to time, but there were, only nine, count 'em, nine days left.

Help was on its way

45. *March 22, 2014*

My resources were being seriously challenged. I had been spending more on lodging than I had planned. I had not been reaching out to many Legion and VFW posts. I was tired, my spirits were low, and I was avoiding as much interaction as possible while still getting the job done.

Enter Deanah "Sassy D" Hendrix into my life. A long time FB friend, Deanah is well connected to the veteran community in North Carolina and offered to fill up my "dance card" while in the state. It didn't quite work out completely, but well enough, and I was able to stay with her for a night before moving through the state, meeting some other wonderful and dedicated veterans.

Deanah is a wonderful and inspirational example of those who serve who have never served themselves. Coming from a military family, she understands the needs of the veteran community. And, through her love of motorcycle riding, participates in major rides in the Southeast like the Tour of Honor, raising funds for Fisher House, an organization that provides nearby housing for a loved one in the event of a veteran's illness, disease or injury. Thank God for people like Deanah working for all of us.

Near Camp Lejeune, in Jacksonville, North Carolina, construction was taking place on an expansion to the existing Vietnam veterans' memorial. I had seen only a concept drawing of the proposed addition, which was an open circle with Grecian columns around the perimeter. By the time of my visit it had come to partial life with the addition of a dome covering and connecting the columns, and a wider perimeter of curved glass barriers engraved with the names of North Carolina's fallen. I hope to get back there once it is finished. I am convinced it will become one of the most visited memorials of the era.

Fayetteville was a feast. Two separate and distinct memorials dotted the city. There is a generic veterans' memorial that was anything but generic. Huge symbols spelling out the many virtues of our military through the years with stunning modern art installations interpreting each of those virtues in a unique manner. I was hosted that evening by Marie and her husband, both veterans, and enjoyed dinner and conversation with them before turning in.

In Charlotte, my host and friend, John Coulombe, checked me into a really nice hotel. We shared a meal before agreeing to meet the next morning at the Mecklenburg County Vietnam Veterans' Memorial in Thompson Park. I found a sweeping wall honoring those KIA in Vietnam from their county. John, former Army Airborne, had some stories to tell, and I enjoyed my time with him before needing to push on.

The next two days took me to several smaller memorials at various county seats in North Carolina. Passing through the very small town of China Grove, I had difficulty in locating the memorial. In Hannah Park, barely large enough to be called a park, I found the memorial at the very back, between a hedgerow of bushes in front of the creek that runs behind the main street. The modest brickwork and flagpole, with its lush backdrop, is an endearing tribute to the three boys from China Grove who perished In Country.

The following day took me through Yadkinville and Winston Salem, a visit to a beautifully designed but badly deteriorating memorial in Greensboro and on to Wentworth for the night. With only five more days of travel ahead of me, I was excited the next morning and looking forward to meeting a FB friend at the memorial in Durham, which also turned out to be the last really good day on the road. OB Jammer, his Facebook name, is a very active and vocal supporter of veterans' causes.

> *OB is an Air Force veteran who never stopped taking care of other vets, whether by volunteering at the Durham VA hospital, speaking about his experiences, or riding with the CVMA, the Patriot Guard Riders or attending Rolling Thunder. He is out there doing what he can. You are appreciated more than you know, OB.*

The memorial in Durham was set back from the road in a very pastoral setting. It reminded me a little of the Portland, Oregon memorial, but more closed in and intimate. Nestled in a small opening in the lodge pole pine forest, the memorial radiated symbolism and brotherhood in its simple, yet bold design. Adjacent to it was a smaller memorial to Bernie, a War

Dog, with details about the Dog Soldiers of Vietnam not generally known:

> *Over 4000 Canine Soldiers Served in Vietnam…281 dogs*
> *Were officially listed a Killed in Action…only about*
> *200 of the dogs that served were returned to the U.S.*
>
> *It is estimated that these dogs and their handlers*
> *saved over 10,000 lives*

> …SSgt Donnie Taylor,
> Bernie's Handler

After lunch, OB and I went to downtown Raleigh for a visit to the North Carolina Vietnam Veterans' Memorial. We found a major sculpture featuring three life-sized bronzes of soldiers on patrol: one wounded and supported by a buddy scanning the sky for their evac chopper, and the other at the ready, attentive for what the next few seconds might bring. I know this seems a bit clichéd by now, what seems a similar tribute in many places around the country, but it reinforces the idea of teamwork and brotherhood among those who were in the thick of the action, and whose very hopes and lives rested on the soldier next to them. It is always moving to witness.

* * * * *

Three days to go.

I pushed on into Louisburg on my way into Kinston, North Carolina, and an improbable band of brothers. Kinston is a small town a little north and east of Fayetteville. I encountered some very big hearts there. The city was home to two separate memorials and my host, Eric Cantu, made sure I saw everything the town offered before taking me to the new space they were slowly turning into a museum of the Vietnam experience. These dedicated men all want to leave something behind them, and their military living history museum fits the bill perfectly. While there, I was introduced to Murphy's Laws of Combat, some of which are:

1. You are not Superman.
2. If it's stupid but it works, it's not stupid.
3. If you are short of everything except enemy, you are in combat.
4. If the enemy is in range, so are you.
5. Anything you do can get you shot, including doing nothing.
6. Professional soldiers are predictable, but the world is full of amateurs.
7. Murphy was a grunt.

There are more than twenty other insights in Murphy's Laws of Combat, but you get the drift. Not bad lessons to learn for real life, either.

I'd like to say I was the life of the party, the center of attention, but it just wasn't happening for me. I was beyond tired, beyond being able to show or share any real feeling, and, during lunch with the guys, was barely able to keep my head up and speak in whole sentences. I was done; just couldn't quite admit it to myself.

The next-to-last day of the Tour found me moving quickly through Rocky Mount and Elizabeth City, to my final night on the road in Virginia Beach. It rained most of the day and well into the evening. I had a nice room on an upper floor of a hotel, with a great balcony looking out over the beach and the gunmetal grey of the ocean. I took a short walk out to the beach and got my feet wet, but my heart wasn't really in it. I went back to the room, changed, went out to dinner, came back and crashed early. And it was a good day compared to what I woke up to the next morning.

The Last Day. No memorials to see. Nobody I needed to talk to. No interviews to give. No photos to take. Just about 200 miles of highway separating me from Jan's house in Falls Church and the finish line. After my previous visit last July, Jan invited me back to decompress from the journey, understanding even then, much more clearly than I, how necessary that time would be.

It was still raining, harder now and colder than the day before. I had a quiet breakfast, packed up and left the beach. March 30th…more winter than spring. Heading back to Richmond, it just got colder and colder and the rain morphed into a freezing drizzle. Somewhere north of Richmond it turned to a sleet storm and, about fifty miles from Falls Church, into a full-on blizzard. I wanted to cry. I just wanted to pull to the side of the road and never move again. The road got worse and the traffic heavier the closer I came to the metro DC area. I was talking to myself, arguing with myself, screaming to myself, all the way into Jan's driveway. When I stopped the car, turned off the ignition, I sat in silence for a few minutes, trying to become fully human again, or as close as I could muster. It was done.

Aftermath

Jan was the perfect hostess. She left me alone and let me come back to real life on my own terms. I was able to talk in complete sentences after only two days and got more sociable. Frank and I managed to go out and visit a couple of memorials that I missed on my previous visit. I was invited to lunch at the offices of United Charitable Programs, and together we celebrated the end of my journey.

I was able to explore the city at will and actually enjoy myself for the first time in longer than I even wanted to guess. It was good. We went to several ethnic restaurants in the area, watched her son play soccer, went to church together, did stuff and just got along really well.

I loved being there with the two of them in her great home and her two amazing dogs, but everything must end. After nine incredibly restful days, it was time to head west once again.

I have no recollection at all where I spent that first night on the way home, but the second night was another opportunity to visit Francine and Bill in Nashville.

I did something different the following night in Cape Girardeau, Missouri. I actually slept in my car for the first time of the entire journey. I found a campground open in the middle of town and rented a space. I had packed everything I needed to be comfortable in the car if necessary but had never needed any of it. A thick tri-fold mat, sleeping bag, blankets and a pillow made up my bed for the night, and I actually enjoyed it.

Farther south and west took me to Oklahoma City and a visit to the memorial of the 1995 bombing…a huge, open, visceral monument to the lives lost in that fateful incident.

I cruised north from OKC to Winfield, Kansas, for the second time to have another beer with Steven Markley. He was the only one of three veterans I interviewed during that first week that I was able to reconnect with.

On the road that last day, April 15, 2014, I had lunch in Dodge City, turned right to I-70, and was on cruise control all the way back to Denver. I was almost home.

The people renting my home had six weeks remaining on the lease; weeks that were cut out of the tour due to weather and other considerations, and I was able to enjoy the hospitality of friends, first about ten days with my friend Lee, and the rest with another friend, Patti Carpenter, Then, I was really home.

So, was it worth it? Absolutely. I saw things I never imagined. I had my preconceptions shattered on a regular basis, causing me to look more closely at each experience and to see without judgment. I rekindled many old friendships, created new ones and spent time with family around the country that I had missed, sometimes for decades. And I think I opened some eyes and created some awareness of the organizations I supported and will continue to support.

I found generous hearts in many parts of the country and support from many disparate sources. This is something I could never have done alone. I felt blessed each and every day on the road.

Gradually, life became normal again. I went back to the VA seeking help with various ailments. I sought out other friends to reconnect with, and spent time at church, immersing myself back into my spiritual groove.

Today, one full year after my return to Denver, life is as good and as different as it is possible to be. By the end of 2014 I was stable and productive, back to work with the company I left to pursue this dream, and having just completed my first draft of this book.

In January, I met the love of my life and we became engaged barely a month later. In March, following the collapse of the company I had returned to, I was basically retired for the third time. In April I sold my house and I am now living in a different city with a wonderful woman and life has never been better.

In my mind I am completely unrecognizable from the person who returned to Denver only a short time ago, a little broken, exhausted, awed by my experiences and grateful to all who played a part in this great adventure.

Remember

If you are able,
save for them a place
inside of you.

And save one backward glance
when you are leaving for the places they can no longer go.

Be not ashamed to say that you loved them,
though you might not have, always.

Take what they have left,
and what they have taught you
with their dying,
and keep it your own.

And in a time
when men decide and feel safe
to call war insane,
take one moment to embrace
those gentle heroes
you left behind.

Major Michael Davis O'Donnell, Helicopter Pilot
January 1, 1970
KIA March 24, 1970, Dak To, Vietnam

Special Thanks to:

Ginger Campbell, Snap Productions, Los Angeles, CA…whose early guidance and support made much of what followed possible. Snap productions is a full-service event coordination and public relations company.

Maryann Brown, Creative Marketing Café, Denver, CO…whose web site gave me instant credibility and showed the world what I intended to accomplish with this Tour.

United Charitable Programs, Falls Church, VA…whose special knowledge and attention to financial details kept me from going off the rails, and provided needed support several times along the way. Experts in philanthropy, they oversaw the administrative, legal and tax-based aspects of the Tour.

Brand Agents, Denver, CO…whose prompt attention to my needs kept those Tour hats coming, allowing me to keep raising donations. Their expansive catalog of all things embroidable and affordable provided me with much-needed resources along the way.

Tamara Heater, STRM Media-Select LLC, Fort Lauderdale, FL...whose knowledge of interactive web processes allowed me to expand the nature of my Internet presence in ways that are still a mystery to me.

Rev. Dr. Roger Teel, Mile Hi Church of Religious Science, Lakewood, CO...whose faith in my mission, and willingness to support it through introductions to like-minded Centers for Spiritual Living around the United States, insured I would be warmly received by people all over the country... a pearl of great price for certain.

Banner Signs and Graphics, Lakewood, CO...whose artistry and generosity gave my Tourmobile a classic look and feel. With the Tour logos abaft and abeam, I had a unique presence on the roads of America, all through that year on the road.

Tucker Smallwood, Reseda, CA, Actor and Veteran Advocate...whose deeds were an inspiration to me and an indication of what could be done and what must be done for our veterans, and whose earlier comments are indispensible to this work.

Acknowledgments

I wish to thank the following for their support along the way. The people provided shelter, financial contributions, an occasional meal and guidance along the way. Without any one of you this journey would not have turned out as it did. I have undoubtedly left out some people owing to my imperfect notes or illegible handwriting. Please know, if you are not on this list, you are still in my heart and my gratitude flows to you always.

Adele Gondjian
Adjutant Louis Krueger, Centralia, IL
Affordable Auto Repair, Denver, CO
Alan and Cheryl Kuentz
Alejandro Sifuentes
Alexander Wasserman and Jessica Oudin
American Dream Mortgage, Lakewood, CO
American Legion Post 178, Lakewood, CO
Anahid and Dianna Varadian
Anthony and Brelinda Kern
Ardyce West
Barbara Barber
Beverly Sparks

Bill Freeman

Bill Wright, VFW Post 4088, Mark Twain Lake, MO

Bob and Kelly Starry

Bob Bigley

Bob and Debbie McLaughlin

Brian and Christina Bettes

Bruce and Barbara Albert

Bruce and Barbara Brunson

Carol and Ron Colucci

Carol Fulfer

Carolyn Blashek

Charlene Bragg

Charles Hicks

Christine Koch

Christine Lukasic

Christopher Tucker

Claudia Hardesty

Cdr Anthony Gibson, VFW Post 8773, Junction City, KS

Cdr Barbara Aguirre, AL Post 100, Rogers AR

Cdr Bill Ascue, AL Post 9, Bluefield, WV

Cdr Bill Humphrey, VFW Post 3838, Cape Girardeau MO

Cdr Bob McCue, AL Post 447, Mt Pulaski, IL

Cdr Bob Sarver, VVA Post 913, Branson, MO

Cdr Doug Klouse, VFW Post 2590 Carthage, MO

Cdr Gary Lowe, VFW Post 4116, Rogue River, OR

Cdr James Dothrow, VFW Post 4176, Montgomery, AL

Cdr John Paynter, AL Post 218, Middletown, OH

Cdr Larry Wood AL Post 12, Vienna, MO

Cdr Murry Kachel, AL Post 595, Del Rio, TX

Cdr Pete Regules, AL Post 29, Zanesville, OH

Cdr Randy English, VFW Post 972, Terre Haute, IN

Cdr Terry McGuinness, AL Post 649, Blessing, TX

Colon Laney

Dan Kirkpatrick

Dan Lundin

Dan Ninedorf

Daniel Komer

Danny and Lori Ley Strickland

David Goode

Debbie Koebel

Deanah Hendrix

Diane and Scott Dantema

Dick and Barbara Riegler

Don and Kay Norton

Dr. Beth Jewett

Ed Brake

Eileen Kennedy

Elmer Everetts, VFW Post 844, Williamsport, PA

Eric Cantu, VVA Post 892, Kinston, NC

Fidelity Charitable Gift Fund, Denver, CO

Francine Kline and Bill Clark

Francis Ormsbee, Service Officer, AL Post 21, Newport, VT

Frank Ashinhurst

Frank Clark

Frank Kotlarz

Gary and Peggy Heligman

Gary Eisenhower

Glen and Sandra Harrop

Geoffrey Oshman

Harry Gross

Hostel Boise www.hostelboise.com

James Helmkamp

Jan Ridgely

Jerry Blake

Jerry Lawson

Jerry Penrod, Quartermaster. AL Post 210, Danville, IL

Jim Ewen

Jim Lutz

Jim O'Brien

Jim Reis

Jim Rippy, VFW Post 4398, Richmond, MO

Joe and Barbara Fischer

Joe Kopacz

John and Kathleen Miller

John Beadle and Noreen

John Coulombe

John Hanson, VFW Post 5040, Woodstock, IL

John Kustafik

Katie Luckett

Kelly Bohm

Kris Kirkorian

L Nolte, Amvets

Larry and Tryna Cooper

Larry Disher

Larry Lee Jr

Larry Stimeling

Lee Cuccinela

Leianna Roup

Les Bryan

Leslie Lassi

Linda Betz

Linda McDonald

Lou Halverson

Lowell Swindler, Jr.

Lynn Gustafson Fulton

Manoog Kaprelian

Marie Kirkland

Mark and Maryann Cullin

Mark Kramer

Mark Walker, AVVBA, Atlanta, GA

Marvin Hume

Maureen Underwood

Merrick Labor
Michael Enquis
Mike and Pat Gostanian
Mike Kirkorian
Mike Doak
Nikki Campbell-Smith
OB Jammer
Pam Fagelson
Pamela Willett
Paracord Ron
Patti Carpenter
Paul and Barbara Snow
Paul and Helen Gabriel
Paul and Lori Reader
Patricia Evans
Polly Letofsky
Radine Coopersmith and Jerry Stang
Ralph Dyson
Randy Hood
Ray Hildreth
Rev Barbara Jefferys, CSL Sylva, NC
Rev Celeste Frazier, Du Page CSL, Lisle, IL
Rev Chris Michaels, Spirit of Kansas City CSL, Kansas City, KS
Rev Jesse Jennings, CSL Houston, TX
Rev June Clark, Miracle CSL, Cleveland, OH
Rev Joann McFadden, Charlton, NY
Rev Marigene de Rusha, CSL St. Louis, MO
Rev Patrick and Susan Pollard, CSL Middletown, CT
Ric Harshman
Richard Farhat
Richard Smith
Robert and Theresa Slusher
Ron "Pops" Reilly
Ronald and Suzi Miulli

Rudy Paszkiewicz
Scott and Angie Vermillion (and kids)
Simon Moore
Spencer Bumgardner
Stanley Odle
Stephen G Wheeler
Steve Kindsfather
Steve Steinhouse
Sue Hoffman Margolis
Sue Mitchell Snyder
Terri Shelefontiuk
The Little Café, Encino, CA
Tim O'Rourke
Tom Smith
Tom Suprock
Vicky Davey
Vikki Carter
Walter Curry
Wayne Smith
Whit Goddard
William and Susan Loving
Willis Harding

Veterans Organizations Worth Your Support

Operation First Response: This organization supports our nation's wounded warriors and their families' personal and financial needs. Services are provided from the onset of injury, throughout the recovery period and along the veteran's journey from military to civilian life. They also offer funds for utilities, rent, vehicle payments, groceries, clothing and travel expenses. www.operationfirstresonse.com

The Soldiers Project: Supports veterans afflicted with PTSD with free, confidential psychological counseling. They extend these services to their families and loved ones as well.
www.thesoldiersproject.org

Transitioning Veteran: Assists veterans separating from the active military and settling into civilian life, primarily through employment assistance and information on veteran's benefits. www.transitioningveteran.com

Soldiers Angels: An organization that provides aid and comfort to the men and women of all service branches, their families and the growing veteran population in a variety of creative and needed ways. www.soldiersangels.org

Veteran Homestead: Based in Fitchburg, MA, this organization provides housing and care to U.S. Armed Services Veterans who are elderly, disabled or have been diagnosed with a terminal illness.
www.veteranhomestead.org

Blinded Veterans Association: Through their service programs, regional groups, resources and advocacy before the legislative and executive branches of government, they strive to make life better for blinded veterans.
www.bva.org

Veterans Dream Foundation: This organization works with donors and other organizations to fulfill the final wishes of terminally ill veterans. These veterans' final wishes have included everything from fulfilling basic needs (like a working appliance or mobility scooter) to arranging bedside reunions, final vacations with family, "meet and greets" with personal heroes or opportunities to reconnect with aspects of former military service.
www.dreamfoundation.org

The Twilight Brigade: is one of the largest end-of-life care communities operating as an independent agency within VA hospitals and hospices across America. Their 5000+ volunteers are dedicated to being at the bedsides of our nation's dying veterans. www.thetwilightbrigade.com

The F7 Group: This Texas-based organization is dedicated to empowering female veterans by providing resources, training and support to women transitioning from the military back into an enriching and fulfilling civilian life. www.f7group.com

Vietnam Specific Memorials in the U.S.

Alabama:

Allgood: Allgood Fire Station, SH 75 & Godfrey Dr
Anniston: Centennial park
Athens: Welcome Center, I-65 & County Road 144
Clanton: Courthouse Grounds, 2nd Ave N & 6th St N
Cullman: Cullman County Courthouse, 6th St SW & 1st Ave SW
Dalesville: Fort Rucker, US Army Aviation Museum
Decatur: Veterans Park, Cain St NE & Ferry St NE
Gadsden: Noccalula Fall Park, Woodcliff & Body Sts
Mobile: Battleship Park, Multiple Exhibits,
Battleship Pkwy & Old Spanish Trail
Oneonta: Memorial Highway Median, SH 75 & 3rd Ave W
Prattville: Courthouse Grounds, W 4th& S Court Sts
Tallassee: Central Blvd & Freeman Ave
Wetumpka: Elmore County Courthouse, S Main & Commerce Sts

Arizona:

Bullhead City: Arizona Veterans Memorial Park, Colorado River
Casa Grande: Reed-Mashore Muni. Park, E 4th.& N. Picacho Sts

Flagstaff: Wheeler Park, W Birch Ave & N Kendrick St

Fountain Hills: Veterans Plaza. E. Scottsdale, E El Lago Dr& E Kiwanis Dr

Kingman, Railroad Park, 315 W Beale St

Lake Havasu City: Wheeler Park, N. McCulloch Blvd at Civic Center Ln.

Phoenix: Wesley Bolin Memorial Park, W Jefferson St & N 7th Ave

Sierra Vista: Cochise College Campus, N Colombo Ave & Campus Drive

Tucson: El Presideo Plaza, W Pennington St

Arkansas:

Blytheville: County Courthouse, N 3rd& W Walnut Sts

Clinton: Van Buren County Courthouse, Elm & Griggs Sts

Fort Smith: Sebastian County Courthouse, 6th St & Parker Ave

Little Rock: State Capitol, Woodlane St & W 6th Ave

Morrilton: Conway County Courthouse, S Moose & E Church Sts

Paris: Courthouse Lawn, W Walnut St & S Express St

Rogers: Rogers Airport, NE Hudson Rd & Happy Trails Dr

Searcy: White County Courthouse, W Race Ave & N Spruce St

Van Buren: Main & 4thSts

California:

Anderson: Shasta 7 W Center Sts

Azusa: Civic Center, E Foothill Blvd & N Dalton Ave

Bakersfield: Courthouse Plaza, Truxtun & N Chester Aves

Barstow: Main Street & N. 3rd Ave

Berkeley: Veterans Memorial Building, 1931 Center St

Burbank: McCambridge Park, 1515 N Glenoaks Blvd.

Carlsbad: Carlsbad Blvd & Cypress Ave

Carmel: Devendorf Park, Mission St & 12th Ave

Chiriaco Summit: Patton Museum, I-10 and Summit Rd

Coachella: Vietnam Veterans Park, 4th St & Orchard St

Colton: Fleming Park, West F St and La Cadena Dr

Concord: Memorial Grove, Turtle Creek & Swallow Tail Rds
Coronado: Naval Amphibious Base, USN & Coast Guard Memorial
    Tulagi Rd and Rendova Circle
Cupertino: Memorial Park, Stevens Creek Bl and Patriot Way
Fresno: Lao Hmong memorial, Fresno St & Van Ness Ave
Grass Valley: Route 20/49 Bridge at Colfax Ave
Grass Valley: Brunswick Road, Bridge over S H 49
Grass Valley: Dorsey Drive Bridge, over SH 49
Grass Valley: Maryland Road, over SH 49
Grass Valley: Bennett Street, over SH 49
Grass Valley: Empire Street, over SH 49
Grass Valley: Bank Street& SH 49 Frontage Rd
Grass Valley: Mill Street & McCourtney Rd
Grass Valley: Banner Lava Cap Road, over SH 49
Grass Valley: Memorial Park, Memorial Lane & Race St
Guadelupe: 890 Guadelupe (Hwy 1) across from Santa Florita Hotel
Hayward: Lonetree Cemetery, Hansen Rd & Fairview Ave
Hollister: Veterans Hall, San Benito & 7th St
King City: King City High School, Co Rd G13 & N Mildred Ave
La Fayette: Veterans Memorial Bldg, Mt. Diablo Blvd & Risa Rd
La Mesa: Crossroads Shopping Center, University Ave and 13A
Livermore: Carnegie Park, S. J St. & 4th Ave
Lompoc: River Park, River Park Rd
Long Beach: Houghton Park, Atlantic Ave& E Harding St
Los Angeles: Civic Center Courtyard, N Broadway &
    W Temple St
Los Angeles: Japanese-American Cultural &Community Center
    San Pedro St & W. 3rd St
Los Osos: Los Osos Memorial Park, Sombrero Dr& Los Osos
    Valley Rd
Marina del Rey: Dedicated Vietnam Veterans Memorial Highway
Milpitas: Mipitas Civic Center Vietnam Memorial,
    Town Center Drive & N Milpitas Blvd
Mission Viejo: Community Center, Veterans Way

Monrovia: Monrovia Library, 321 S Myrtle Ave

Nevada City: Washington Street Bridge, over SH 49

Nevada City: Sacramento Street Bridge, over SH 49

Nevada City: Broad Street Bridge, over SH 49

Nevada City: Gold Run Road, Bridge over SH 49

Nevada City: Pioneer Park, Nile & Nimrod Sts

North Hollywood: Valhalla Memorial Park, 10621 Victory Blvd

Novato: Novato High School, Arthur & Hayes Sts

Palm Desert: Civic Center Park, Fred Waring Drive &
    San Pablo Ave

Palm Desert: El Paseo & Plaza Way

Pasadena: Pasadena Memorial Park, 85 E Holly St

Petaluma: Walnut Park, Petaluma Blvd S & E St

Pittsburg: Small World Park, Harbor St & Leland Lane

Porterville: Veterans Park, W Henderson Ave & N Newcomb St

Rancho Cucamonga: Alta Loma High School, 8880 Baseline Rd

Redwood City: City Hall, Middlefield Rd & Jefferson Ave

Riverside: March AFB Parade Ground, Baucom & Dekay Aves

Riverside: March AFB…War Dog memorial

Rohnert Park: Sonoma State University Campus, W Redwood Dr &
    Vine St

Roseville: Saugstad Park, Franklin St & Douglas Blvd

Sacramento: California State Capitol, 15th& L Sts

Sacramento: Mather Field, VA Medical Center,
    Peter A McCuen Blvd & Buffington St

Salinas: Salinas Soccer Field Complex, Constitution Blvd & E
    Laurel Dr

San Diego: Inspiration Point, Balboa Park, Chapel Rd &Stitt Ave

San Francisco: The Presidio of San Francisco, Ord St & Infantry Ter-
    race

San Francisco: Pier 45, Merchant Marine Memorial, Fisherman's
    Wharf

San Jose: Oak Hill Memorial Park, Curtner Ave & SH 82

San Jose: Guadalupe River Park, Delmas Ave & W Santa Clara St

San Juan Capistrano: San Juan Creek, Calle Perfecto & Valle Rd

San Mateo: Fire Headquarters, S Ellsworth & 1st Aves

San Pedro: South Harbor Bl and 6th St

San Raphael: Avenue of the Flags, Civic Center Dr&
    Avenue of the Flags

Santa Barbara: Elings Park, Las Positas Rd and
    Jerry Harwin Pkwy

Santa Maria: Simas Park, Boone& McClelland Sts

Seal Beach: Eisenhower Park, Ocean Ave & Seal Beach
    Municipal Pier

Solana Beach: Solana Beach Plaza, HWY 101 &
    Lomas Santa Fe Dr

Sonora: Sonora Veterans Museum, E Jackson St & SH 49

Stockton: Martin Luther King Jr. Plaza, E Oak & N Center Sts

Torrance: Courthouse/Library Complex, Maple Ave &
    Torrance Blvd

Tulare: Meffort Field Airport, Tex Dr& E Rankin Rd

Vacaville: City Hall, Merchant St & Walnut Ave

Venice: Wall of Honor for POW/MIAs, Ocean Ave

Visalia: Convention Center, S Bridge St & E Acequia Ave
    (Courtyard Alcove)

Walnut Creek: City Hall, N Main St & Civic Dr

Westminster: Sid Goldstein Freedom Park, Monroe and 13thSts

Willows: Clock Plaza, Tehama & E Walnut Sts

Woodlake: Community Park, E Naranjo Blvd & N Magnolia St

Yountville: Veteran Home Chapel, President's Circle &
    California Dr

Colorado:

Boulder: Municipal Building, 1777 Broadway

Boulder: Boulder Creek Trail

Colorado Springs: Prospect Lake Memorial Park, Multiple Displays
    Pikes Peak Ave & S Union Blvd

Cripple Creek: Bennett Ave & Carhanate St

Florence: Fremont County Airport, Decker & Shoop Drs

Fruita/Gr. Junction: Vietnam Veterans Memorial State Park,
I-70 and Exit 19

Ft. Collins: Colorado State University Campus, Meridian Ave &
North Dr

Greeley: Weld County Veterans Memorial Plaza, Lincoln Park,
35th Ave & W 16th St

Longmont: Jim's Pond, Co Rd 1 & E 17th Ave

Longmont: Nature Preserve, Co Rd 1 & E 17th Ave

Pueblo: Pueblo City Park, N Elizabeth & W 26thSts

Trinidad: Colorado Welcome Center, N Animas St & Nevada Ave

Connecticut:

Bloomfield: Bloomfield Town Green, Bloomfield & Park Aves

Coventry: Veterans Memorial Green, Cross & High Sts

Danbury: Memorial Drive off I-84

Gaylordsville: Gaylord School, Church & Cedar Hill Rds

Granby: Town Common, Salmon Brook St & Hartford Ave

Hartford: City Hall Park, Fairfield & New Britain Aves

Manchester: Main Street

New Britain: Willowbrook Park

New Fairfield: Brush Hill Road

New Haven: Vietnam Veterans memorial Park, I-95 and exit 46

New London: USCG Academy, behind chapel, Tampa &
Harriet Lane

Norwich: Chelsea Parade North, I/S of Washington St & Broadway
Torrington: Coe Memorial Park, Litchfield & Summer Sts

Trumbull: Intersection of Highways 125 & 25

Wallingford: 1151 E Center St

Windsor Locks: Memorial Hall, Elm & S Main Sts

Delaware:

Dover: North of Dover AFB, County Drive & County Rd 67

Wilmington: Brandywine Park, Baynard Blvd & N Park Dr

Florida:

Belleview: 5400 Block of Abshier Blvd

Bradenton: Courthouse, Manatee Ave W & 12th St W

Crestview: Crestview High School, SH 85 & Garden St

DeLand: Veterans Plaza, N Florida & E Indiana Aves

Dunedin: Dunedin Memorial Stadium, CR 99 & McLean St

Fort Meade: City Hall, N Charleston Ave & County Road 630

Fort Walton Beach: Eglin AFB, 2nd St & Chinquapin Dr

Gainesville: Old Courthouse Grounds, NE 1st St & SE 1st Ave

Key West: Bayview Park, Truman Ave & Eisenhower Dr

Lake City: Olustee Park, NE Hermando Ave & NW Madison St

Melbourne: DAV of Melbourne, Varnum St & Highland Ave

Milton: Santa Rosa County Veterans Memorial Plaza, Oak &
    Willing Sts

Ocala: Marion County Veterans Memorial Park, E Fort King St & SE
    26th Terrace

Ocean City: Hurlburt Field Special Operations Squadron,
    Several Exhibits, Cody Ave & US 98

Pensacola: Veterans Memorial Park, Multiple Installations
    Bayfront Pkwy & E Romana St

Perry: Veterans Memorial Park, N Washington & W Margurite Sts

Port St. Lucie: Veterans Memorial Park, River Aquatic Preserve

Sebastian: Riverview Park, Sebastian Blvd EB & Indian River Dr

Tallahassee: State Capitol Complex, S Monroe & E Madison Sts
    Tarpon Springs: Craig Park, S Spring & Bath Sts

Valparaiso: Eglin AFB, Eglin Blvd & Pinchot Rd

Vero Beach: Veterans Memorial Island Sanctuary

Georgia:

Atlanta Area: 23 individual plaques scattered around the city

Atlanta: Georgia Tech Campus, North Ave NW &Techwood Dr
    Atlanta Woodward Academy

Atlanta: Georgia War Veterans Memorial Complex, Capitol Ave SE &
    Martin Luther King Jr Dr SE

Bowdon: Park on East College St., City Hall Ave & Wood Alley

Brunswick: Glynn County Courthouse, G & Ellis Sts

Columbus: Vietnam Veterans Memorial Park, Buena Vista Rd &
    Lawyer's Lane

Cordele: Veterans Memorial State Park off Cannon Rd.

Donaldsonville: Seminole County Courthouse, S Knox Ave &
    W 2nd St

Gainesville: Rock Creek Park, Northside Dr & Academy St

Gainesville: Bradford St N & Spring St NE

Griffin: Stonewell Cemetery, Memorial Dr& E Taylor St

Hartwell: Hart County Courthouse, W Franklin St & N Forest Ave

Roswell: Memorial Gardens, N Atlanta & Hill Sts

Savannah: Emmet Park, E Bay & Price Sts

Smyrna: 2800 King St

Hawaii:

Hilo: Wailoa River Park, Pauahi St and Piopio St

Honolulu: Punchbowl Nat. Cemetery, Iolani Ave & Prospect St

Honolulu: State Capitol Grounds, Richards & S Hotel Sts

Honolulu: Fort Shafter, off Likelike Hwy

Idaho:

Coeur d'Alene: Veterans Memorial Park, Civic Center

Idaho Falls: Freeman Park, Baseball & Micro Sts

Kuna: Colonel Bernard Fisher Veterans Memorial Park,
    W 3rd St & Ave A

Mountain Home: Mountain Home AFB, Grandview Road

Mullan: Earl & 2nd St

Nampa: Inside City Hall, 3rd St S & 5th Ave S

Nampa: Outside City Hall, 3rd St S & 5th Ave S

Twin Falls: City Park, Shoshone St & 4th Avenue E

Illinois:

Calumet City: River Oaks Dr& Wentworth Ave

Carthage: Adjacent to the Kibbe Museum, Main & N Fayette Sts

Centralia: Fairview Park, Multiple Exhibits, W Broadway & County View

Chicago: Veterans Art Museum, 1801 S Indiana Ave

Chicago: Wabash Plaza, W Lake St & N Dearborn St

Chicago: Survivors Memorial, 815 S. Oakley Blvd. W Polk St & S Oakley Blvd

Flora: Public Library, N Main & W 3rdSts

Freeport: Stevenson County Courthouse, Galena and Stevenson Sts

Freeport: All Veterans Memorial Park, Lamm & Walnut Rds

Havana: Courthouse Lawn, W Market & N Plum Sts

Jacksonville: Nichols Park, Hollkenbrink Dr

Lansing: Lansing Municipal Airport, Lansing Rd & Burnham Ave

Macomb: 1800 E University Dr

Metropolis: Massac County Courthouse Grounds, Market St & W 5th Ave

Mounds: VFW Lawn, Old US Hwy 51 & 3rd St

Mt. Pulaski: Town Square, N Washington St & E Jefferson St

Mulberry Grove: School Lawn, W Wall & 7thSts

Rock Island: National Cemetery, Burr Dr& Rodman Ave

Rockford: Midway Village, 6799 Guilford Rd

Skokie: The Wall USA, Community Park, Oakton St & Kenton Ave

Springfield: Oakridge Cemetery, J David Jones Pkwy & Yates Ave

Tilton: Tilton School, W 5th& S H Sts

Waukegan: Veterans Park, Washington & S West Sts

Wheaton: Memorial Park, W Union Ave & N Hale St

Woodstock: McHenry County Administration Building, Ware Rd

Indiana:

Auburn: DeKalb County Courthouse Rotunda

Brazil: Clay County Courthouse, E National Ave & S Alabama St

Bedford: Lawrence County Courthouse Rotunda

Columbia City: E Van Buren St & Towerview Drive

E Chicago: Veterans Park W 145th St & S Indianapolis Blvd

Evansville: Main Street & SE 7th St
Evansville: Riverfront Esplanade, SE Riverside Dr & Chestnut St
Greenfield: Veterans Park, S State St & E 100 St
Greencastle: Putney County Courthouse grounds
Indianapolis: War Memorial Plaza, N Meridian & W North Sts
La Porte: Soldiers Memorial Park, Lake Shore Dr.& Pine Lake Ave
Lawrenceburg: Ohio River Levee Wall & S Walnut St
Lawrenceburg: Dearborn County Courthouse, W 215 High St
Leroy: Stony Run County Park, 2.5 mi north of town
Marion: Grant County Courthouse, E 3rd& S Adams Sts
Marion: Municipal Building, S Branson & E 4thSts
Michigan City: Greenwood Cemetery
Muncie: Heekin Park, E Memorial Dr& S Madison St
Munster: Community Veterans Memorial Park, 9710 Calumet Ave
Noblesville: Hamilton County Courthouse Square, 8th& Connor Sts
Princeton: Gibson County Courthouse, W. Broadway at N Main Sts
Richmond: Freedom Fountain Plaza, 5th& Main Sts
Rockville: Courthouse Lawn, W Oho & S Market Sts
Sullivan: Sullivan Courthouse grounds
Terre Haute: Vigo County Courthouse Lawn, Ohio & S 3rdSts
Whiting: Schrage Ave & 119th

Iowa:

Cedar Falls: Veterans Memorial Park, Hudson Rd & W 23rd St
Clinton: Clinton County Courthouse, N 2nd St & 6th Ave N
Council Bluffs: Bayliss Park, 1st Ave and Pearl St
Des Moines: Iowa State Capitol, E Court Ave & Dey St
Dubuque: Miller Riverview Park, Admiral Sheehy Drive
Greenfield: Iowa 25, 1 mile S of I-80 (exit 86)
Iowa City: Johnson County Courthouse, E Court & S Clinton Sts
Marshalltown: Iowa Veterans Home, Summit St & Liberty Lane
Red Oak: Fountain Square, E Reed & N 4thSts
Waterloo: Paramount Park, E 5th& Water Sts

Kansas:
Emporia: All Veterans Park, 933 S Commercial St
Girard: Courthouse Square, 111 E Forest
Junction City: Heritage Park, N Washington St & W 5th St
Lawrence: University of Kansas Campus, W Campus Rd & Memorial Drive
Lawrence: Army Reserve Center, Iowa & W 21stSts
Lyndon: Osage County Courthouse Lawn, 717 Topeka Ave
Manhattan: Kansas State University Campus
Merriam: Antioch Park Access Rd
Pittsburg: State Univ. Vets Memorial Amphitheater, 1909 S Rouse
Pleasanton: Pleasanton Cemetery
St Mary's: Highway 24 at the west edge of downtown
Topeka: Garfield Park, Garfield Park & NE Monroe St
Topeka: Washburn University Campus, SW 18th St & SW College Ave
Kansas City: Vietnam Veterans Park, Broadway St & Vietnam Veterans Memorial Drive
Kansas City: Leavenworth Rd & 91st St
Wichita: Veterans Memorial Park, 339 N Greenway
Winfield: Memorial Park, Fuller St & E 9th Ave

Kentucky:
Bardstown: Bardstown Visitor's Center, W Stephen Foster Ave & S Third St
Erlanger: Dixie Highway & Commonwealth Ave
Frankfort: Memorial Park, Vernon Cooper Lane & Coffee Tree Rd
Franklin: Simpson County Park, N St & Filter Plant Rd
Henderson: Central Park, Washington & S Main Sts
Lexington: Government Plaza, S Limestone & E Vine Sts
Madisonville: Hopkins County Courthouse, S Main & W Center Sts
Middlesboro: City Center, Lothbury Ave & 21st St
Mount Sterling: Montgomery County War Memorial Courthouse Broadway & W High St

Oak Grove: War Memorial Grove, Ft Campbell Bl &
     Walter Garrett Ln
Oak Grove: Ft. Campbell, Pratt memorial Museum,
     Missouri Ave & Screaming Eagle Blvd
Paducah: Purchase Area, Washington St & S 6th St
Paris: Bourbon County Courthouse, Main St & Ardery Pl
Russellville: Legion Park, Hopkinsville Rd & U.S. 431
Scottsville: Public Library, S Court & E Locust Sts
Wickliffe: Ballard County Courthouse, 132 N 4th St
Winchester: Clark County Courthouse, Cleveland Ave & Wall St

Louisiana:

Baton Rouge: USS Kidd Veterans Memorial Museum,
     Downtown Baton Rouge
Bossier City: Barksdale AFB, Lindeberg & Security Roads
Houma: Veterans Memorial Park, Little Bayou Black Dr& Polk St
LaFayette: Cajundome, Cajundome Blvd & W Congress St
LaFayette: Veterans Park, Greentree Dr & S Beadle Rd
Lake Charles: Veterans Memorial Park, 326 Pujo St
Metairie: Garden of Memories, Vera Rd & Airline Drive
New Orleans: Median Esplanade, Basin & Iberville Sts
New Orleans: Poydras St, Superdome, Plaza Level
Oakdale: E. 6th Ave. Median, E 6th Ave & 10th St
Ville Platte: Evangeline Parish Courthouse, Court &
     West Magnolia Sts

Maine:

Augusta: Capitol Park, State & Capital Sts
Bangor: Cole Land Transportation Museum, 405 Perry Rd
Orono: Nadeau-Savoy Memorial Park, Essex St & Gould Rd
Rumford: High School Park, River & Bridge Sts

Maryland:

Baltimore: Maryland State Veterans Park (Middle Branch Park)

S Hanover St & Waterview Ave

Cumberland: I-68 Rest Area, I-68 E of Cumberland

Frederick: Courts Square, Memorial Pkwy & W 2nd St

Hancock: War Memorial Plaza, W Main & Tonoloway Sts

Sharpsburg: Town Clock Square, Timber Ridge & Oak Forest Rds

Towson: VV Memorial Fountain, no exact address available

Westminster: Next to County Courthouse, exact location unknown

Massachusetts:

Abington: Richard Fitts Dr

Andover: Town Park, Whittier St & Whittier Ct

Belchertown: Town Common, Main & Jabisch Sts

Beverly: 502 Cabot St

Billerica: VV Memorial Park, Treble Cove Rd fronting the Sherriff's Complex

Boston: Back Bay Fens, Park Drive and Agassiz Rd

Charlestown: Veterans Memorial Hall, Green & High Sts

Chicopee: Memorial Green, Front and Bonneville Sts

Danvers: Town Common, Sylvan & Holten St

Dedham: Brookdale Cemetery, Brookdale Ave & Dominic Ct

Dorchester: Dorchester Bay, William T Morrissey Blvd & Savin Hill Ave

Gardner: City Hall, City Hall Ave & Pleasant St

Hanover: In Front of the Town Hall

Holyoke: Veterans Park, Hampden & Maple Sts

Leominster: Memorial Monument Square, Park & West Sts

Lynn: Traffic Island Park, Street Location TBD

Marblehead: Veterans Park, Pleasant & Essex St

Medford: Roll of Honor Park, Winthrop & Brooks Sts

Middleboro: Town Hall Lawn, South Main & Rock Sts

Middletown: Community Center, S Main & Maple Sts

Needham: 1 Sunset Rd

North Adams: VV Memorial Skating Rink, 1267 S Church St

Quincy: Clock Tower, Victory Rd & Miwra Haul Rd

Saugus: Town Hall, Main St & Central St

South Boston: Independence Square, E Broadway & M St

Southbridge: Intersection Park, Main & Mechanic Sts

Stockbridge: Village Green, Church & Main Sts

Springfield: Court Square, E Court St & E Columbus Ave

Springfield: Winchester Square, State & Catherine Sts

Taunton: Church Square, Church Green & SH 44

Webster: Town hall Courtyard, Main & Lake Sts

W Springfield: Town Common, Elm & Park Sts

Weymouth: Multiple Displays, exact address unknown

Wilmington: Public Library, Middlesex Ave & Wildwood St

Worcester: Green Hill Park, Green Hill Parkway & Rodney St

Michigan:

Adrian: Monument Park, E Maumee & N Center Sts

Bay City: Veterans Memorial Park, JFK Dr& E Thomas St

Cheyboygan: Veterans Park, Court & Fillmore Sts

Coleman: Washington & S. 3rd St

Dearborn: Dearborn City Hall, Michigan Ave & Schaefer Rd

East Pointe: City Complex Grounds, S Gratiot & Evergreen Aves

Garden City: Garden City Hall, Middlebelt & Alvin Sts

Grand Rapids: Gerald R Ford Museum, 303 Pearl St NW

Hartford: Ely Park, Franklin & W Main Sts

Hazel Park: Hazel Park City Hall, John R & W 9 Mile Rds

Midland: Midland Cty Courthouse Grounds, W Main & Gordon Sts

Monroe: Heck Park, Detroit St & Exit 15 (I-75)

Mount Pleasant: Island Park, off N Island Park Drive

Muskegon: Vets Memorial Park Island, between the Causeways

Norton Shores: Hidden Cove Park, Seaway Dr& Grand Haven Rd

Novi: Oakland Hills Cemetery, W 12 Mile and Novi Rds

Petoskey: Pennsylvania Park, Howard & E Mitchell Sts

Potterville: Memorial Park, W Main & N Nelson Sts

Saginaw: Veterans Memorial Plaza, S Washington Ave & Hoyt
Park Upper Dr

St. Joseph: Bluff Park, Lake Blvd & Elm St

Southgate: Southgate memorial Library, Reaume &
Veterans Parkways

Tecumseh: Brookside Cemetery, N Union & Chippewa Sts

Westland: City Hall Grounds, Fort Rd & John F Kennedy Drive

Ypsilanti: Ypsilanti Township Hall, Huron St & Huron River Drive

Minnesota:

Duluth: Lakewalk, I-35 at N 4th Ave E

Little Falls: Minnesota State Veteran's Cemetery, SH 115 &
Co. Hwy 76

Long Prairie: Veterans Park, Central Ave & Todd St N

Mankato: Minnesota State University, E Maywood Ave &
N Ellis Ave

Mankato: Vietnam Memorial Park, Stoltzman Rd &
Rasmussen Woods Rd

Red Wing: John Rich Park, HWY 61 & East Ave

St. Paul: State Capitol, John Ireland Blvd & 12th St W

Winona: Veterans Park, Park Dr& Lake Park Dr

Mississippi:

Ocean Springs: Mississippi Vietnam Veterans Memorial Park
Bienville Blvd & Deena Dr

Missouri:

Albany: Gentry County Courthouse, S Smith & W Wood Sts

Belton: Smoot Peace Park, 16400 N Mullen Rd

Branson: Inside the Uptown Café, Gretna Rd & Cedar St

Buckner: Highway 24 & Hudson

Cape Girardeau: Common Pleas Courthouse Grounds,
Broadway & N Lorimer Sts

Carthage: Central Park, W Chestnut & S Maple Sts

Chillicothe: Livingston County Courthouse Square

Columbia: Boone County Courthouse, E Walnut & N 7thSts

Hannibal: Central Park, Broadway Exd & S 4th St
Lexington: Wentworth Military Academy, 1880 Washington Ave
Mark Twain Lake: Clarence Cannon Dam, S.H. J
Moberly: Rothwell Park, Holman Rd & Rothwell Park Rd
O'Fallon: Dames Park, Hwy P & Dames Park Dr
Richmond: Courthouse Lawn, S Thornton & E N Main Sts
St. Clair: American Legion Post 347, W Gravois Ave & Walnut St
St. James: Missouri Veterans Home, S.H. A & County route 435
St. Louis: War Memorial Court of Honor, downtown St. Louis.
     Market & N 14thSts
St. Peters: Willott & Jungermann Roads
Sedalia: Pettis County Courthouse, S Ohio Ave & W 5th St
Springfield: Missouri Veterans Cemetery, E Kemmling Lane &
     Farm Rd 177
Springfield: Springfield National Cemetery, Glenstone Ave &
     E. Seminole St
Vienna: Maries County Courthouse Lawn, S Main & 4thSts
Wentzville: Firemans Park, W Pearce Blvd & Birch

Montana:

Anaconda: Deer Lodge County Courthouse (Plaque) Main St at
     W. 8th St
Billings: Purple Heart Memorial, Yellowstone County Courthouse
Bozeman: Sunset Hills Cemetery City Offices
Lewistown: Museum Park, E Main St & Ridgelawn Ave
Missoula: Missoula Memorial Rose Garden, E Franklin &
     Blaine Sts

Nebraska:

Kearney: Apollo Park, 6th Ave & W 35th St
Lincoln: Nebraska State Veterans Memorial Garden
     Billy Wolff Trail & Normal Blvd
North Platte: 20th Century Veterans Memorial park, 2811 S Jeffers
Omaha: Memorial park, 60th and Dodge Sts

Sidney: American Legion Park, 11th Ave & Legion Park

Nevada:
Boulder City: Veterans Cemetery, Buchanan Blvd & Georgia Ave
Carlin: Perry Memorial Park, B Street & West Railroad Avenue
Carson City: Mills Park, Palo Verde Dr& Drew Way
Elko: Pine St
Reno: Powning Park, Court & S Virginia Sts, Multiple displays
Virginia City: St. Mary's In the Mountains Cath. Church, E &
    Taylor Sts

New Hampshire:
Berlin: Veterans Memorial Park, Green & Main Sts
Boscawen: State Veterans Cemetery, 110 Daniel Webster Highway
Colebrook: Town Green, Daniel Webster Hwy & Bridge St
Dunbarton Center: Town Hall, Stark Hwy S & Everett Rd
Durham: UNH Memorial Union Bldg, 83 main St
Farmington: American Legion Post 60, N Main & Blouin Sts
Franklin: Veterans Park, Central & S Main Sts
Franklin Falls: Soldier's Hall, Central & Church Sts
Groveton: Town Green, Northern Town, Main & West Sts
Nashua: Memorial Park, Ledge St & N 7th St
Nashua: Deschenes Oval, Main & Canal Sts
New Boston: Davis Scenic Drive, River Rd & Howe Bridge
North Woodstock: Soldiers Park, Daniel Webster &
    Kancamagus Hwys
Portsmouth: Pease International Trade Port

New Jersey:
Berlin: Public Lot, County Rd 561 & Taunton Ave
Burlington: American Legion Post 79, High & Belmont Sts
Butler: Park Place, Main St and Park Place
Cedarbrook: Winslow Township Municipal Building,
    Mays Landing Rd & Braddock Ave

Cherry Hill: Municipal Grounds, Mercer St & Graham Ave

Edison: War Memorial Park, Woodbridge & Dorothy Aves

Elizabeth: Winfield Scott Park, Bridge St & Elizabeth Ave

Holmdel: Meditation Garden, Garden State Parkway &
G.S. Art Center

Holmdel: PNC Bank Arts Center, Garden State Parkway &
G.S. Art Center

Magnolia: Edwin I. Johnson American Legion Post 370,
Warwick Rd N & Brooke Ave

Medford Village: N Main & Bank Sts

Metuchen: Veterans Memorial Park, Lake & Essex Aves

Pennsauken: Cooper River Park, Park Blvd & Donahue Ave

Point Pleasant: Little Silver Lake, Baltimora & Arnold Aves

Pompton Plains: First Reformed Church Cemetery, County Rd 504

Somerdale: Tait VFW Post 7334, Kennedy Blvd & Parkview Ave

Spotswood: American Legion Post 253, Se Voe Ave

Tom's River: Library Park, Washington & Robbins Sts

West Orange: Municipal Building Grounds, Main St. &
Lindsey Ave

Wildwood: Columbus Park, Ocean and Burks Aves

New Mexico:

Albuquerque: Veterans Memorial Park, 1100 Louisiana Blvd

Albuquerque: Sunport Blvd near Alb. International Airport

Angel Fire: Vietnam Veterans Memorial State Park, Country Club
Rd & SH 64

Bernalillo: Sandoval County Courthouse, Camino del Pueblo &
Calle Barrio Nuevo

Carlsbad: Eddy County Courthouse, W Mermod & S Canyon Sts

Gallup: Hillcrest Cemetery, I-40 and Munoz Drive

Grants: Friendship Park, El Morro Rd & W Santa Fe Ave

Farmington: Vietnam Veterans Park

Springer: Former Colfax County Courthouse, Maxwell &
Cimarron Aves

Truth or Consequences: Veterans Memorial Park,   S Broadway &
    Platinum Sts

New York:
    Albany: City Park, Hawk & Elk Sts
    Albany: Law and Justice Building, State & Park Sts
    Belmont: County Courthouse Grounds, Court & Genesee Sts
    Bohemia: Islip McArthur Airport entrance
    Brooklyn: Knights of Columbus Hall, Flatlands Ave & E 40th St
    Brooklyn: Father Kehoe Triangle, Flatlands Ave & Ave M
    Buffalo: Kaisertown Section, Clinton & Kelburn Sts
        Buffalo Naval and Serviceman's Park, Erie & Scott Sts
    Copake : Main Street and County Road 7a
    East Meadow: Eisenhower Park, Multiple Displays Park Blvd &
        Newbridge Ave
    Elmira: Vietnam War Museum, 1200 Davis St
    Farmingville: exit 63, Route 83, Long Island
    Fulton: Fulton War Memorial Building, Lakeside &
        CCW Barrett Drs
    Grafton Lakes: Owen & N Long Pond Rds
    Hadley: Park near Rockwell Falls
    Hamburg: Town Hall, S Park Ave & Norway Pl
    Hicksville: Wagner Funeral Home, Jerusalem Ave & 2nd St
    Highland: Across from Highland Fire District HQ, Milton Ave &
        White St
    Huntington: Hecksher Park, Long Island, Main St & Park Ave
    Katonah: Lasdon Park, Past Orchard Hill Rd (Military Nurses
        Memorial)
    Lockport: Veterans Park, Levan Ave & Massachusetts Ave
    Manhattan: Vietnam Veterans Memorial Plaza, South & Broad Sts
    Massapequa: Massapequa Park, Manhattan Ave & Abbey St
    Newburgh: Leroy and Grand Sts
    North Tonawanda: City Hall, Payne Ave & Thompson St
        Northport: VAMC

Ogdensburg: Groulx Park, Ford & Champlain Sts
Port Jervis: Near Elks Memorial Park, Orchard & Sussex Sts
Queensbury: Adirondack Community College Campus, Cty Rd 7
Riverhead: Town Hall, E Main St & Prospect Pl
Rochester: Highland Park, South & Highland Aves
Rosedale: Queens, NYC, Memphis Ave & 248th St
Salamanca: Memorial Park, Broad & Eagle Sts
Springville: Shuttleworth Park, Woodward Ave & Co. Rd 82
Staten Island: Vietnam Veterans Memorial Park, Manor Rd &
    Maine Ave
Tonawanda: City Hall, Niagara St & Niagara Shore Dr
Troy: Riverside Park, River & Front Sts
West Point: US Military Academy, Mills Rd & Lusk Reservoir
West Seneca: Public Library, Union Rd & Legion Pkwy

North Carolina:

Cary: Veterans Freedom Park, W Durham Rd & N Harrison Ave
Charlotte: Thompson Park, E 3rd St & N Kings Dr
China Grove: Hannah Park, N Main & Patterson Sts
Clinton: Sampson County Courthouse, Wall & W Main Sts
Dallas: Next to Dallas PD, S Gaston & W Main Sts
Durham: Edison Johnson Recreation Center, W Murray Ave &
    Elgin St
Elizabeth City: Pasquotank County Courthouse, E Main &
    N Pool Sts
Fallston: American Legion Grounds, E Independence Blvd &
    Armory Dr
Fayetteville: Ft. Bragg, Reilly St & Longstreet Rd
Fayetteville: Lafayette Cemetery, Rosehill Rd & Ramsey St
Fayetteville: Freedom Memorial Park, Murchison Rd & Bragg Blvd
Gastonia: Lineburger Park, E Garrison Blvd & S Chestnut St
Greensboro: Government Plaza, W Washington & S Green Sts
Hendersonville: North Main Street and 1st Ave W
Jacksonville: Lejeune Memorial Gardens, Hwy 24 and

Montford Point Rd

Kinston: Neuseway Park, N Independence & E King Sts

Laurinburg: Scotland Memorial Library, W Church St &
McLaurin Ave

Lexington: Town Square, N Main & E Center Sts

Lincolnton: County Courthouse, W Main & S Aspen Sts

Louisburg: Franklin County Courthouse, Johnson St Exd & Market

Monroe: Union County Courthouse, Skyway Dr& W Crowell St

Morganton: New Courthouse, N Green & E Meeting St

Raeford: Hoke County Courthouse, Main St & E Edinborough Ave

Raleigh: Old Statehouse, E Edenton & S Wilmington Sts

Rockingham: VFW Grounds, SH 220 & W Broad Ave

Rocky Mount: City Lake, Sunset Ave & N Franklin St

Thomasville: Rest Area on I-85 near mile 100

Waynesville: Haywood County Courthouse

Waynesville: Bethel Middle School, Poindexter & Sonoma Rds

Wentworth: Rockingham County Veterans Park,
Hancock Rd & Bear Branch Trail

Wilmington: Hugh McRae Park, S College Rd & Lake Ave

Winston-Salem: Lawrence Joel Veterans Memorial Coliseum
Deacon Blvd & Shorefair Dr NW

Yadkinville: Yadkin County Courthouse, W main & S State Sts

North Dakota:

Bismark: State Capitol Grounds

New Rockford: Roadside Park, US 231 at 3rd Avenue

Ohio:

Amherst: Amherst Beaver Creek Park, N Lake St & Hwy 2

Cambridge: Guernsey County Courthouse, Wheeling Ave & Southgate Pkwy

Cleveland: Superior Ave, Downtown Cleveland

Clinton: Ohio Veterans Memorial Park, Gold Star Mother   Memorial, Fulton St & W Comet Rd

Columbus: Hall of Fame, 77 S High St
Columbus: Veterans Plaza, 35 S 3rd St
Dayton: Vietnam Veterans Memorial Park, W Stewart St &
 S Patterson Blvd
Fairborn: USAF National Museum, Bong St & Spaatz Circle
Fairborn: Memorial Garden, Bong St & Spaatz Cr
Greenville: Bear's Mill, Bear's Mill Rd & Township Hwy 165
Groveport: Motts Military Museum, Lowery Ct & S Hamilton Rd
Huber Heights: Fire Station, Longford Rd & Brandt Pike
Jefferson: Memorial park, W Jefferson & S Chrstnut Sts
Massillon: Veterans Memorial Park, 1st St SE and
 David Canary Dr SE
Medina: 246 Northland Drive
Middletown: Woodside Cemetery, 1401 S Woodside Blvd
Mount Carmel: Union Township Veterans Park Glen Este, With-
 amsville Rd & Clough Pike
New London: Monument Park, S Main & Kirk Sts
New Philadelphia: County Courthouse, S Broadway & E High Sts
Piqua: Veterans Park, Washington Ave & Broadway St
Sandusky: Veterans Park, Central Ave & W Adams St
Troy: Miami Valley Veterans Museum, 1100 Wayne St
Upper Sandusky: Bicentennial Park, N Sandusky Ave & N 5th St
Wellington: Town Park, Magyar & S Main St
Winchester: Arlington Field of Honor Cemetery SE Expressway
 & Winchester Pike
Zanesville: Riverfront Park, Market St & Zane's Landing Trail

Oklahoma:

Atoka: Courthouse, N Delaware Ave & E Court St
Bethany: Southern Nazarene Univ. Campus Green, N Asbury Ave
 & NW 42nd St
Broken Arrow: Community Center, S Main St & E Mason Dr
Del City: Community Center, SE 15th St & Vicki
Enid: Woodring Airport

Henryetta: Public Library, W Main St & N 6th St

Hugo: Post Office

Hulbert: exact location unknown

Lawton: Elmer Thomas Park, NW Ferris Ave & NW 2nd St

Oklahoma City: SE of State Capitol

Ponca City: War memorial Park, 5th and Highland Sts

Oregon:

Albany: Linn County Park, 900 Price Rd SE

Bend: Deschutes Memorial Garden, The Dalles-California Hwy

Beaverton: Elks Lodge, SW 104th Ave & SW Canyon Rd

Canby: Triangle Park, SW 1st Ave & Birch St

Coos Bay: Mingus Park

Eugene: West Lawn Memorial Park, 225 S Danebo Ave

Eugene: South Eugene HS, 400 E 19th Ave

Grants Pass: Riverside park, 111 E Park St

Hood River: Courthouse, 601 State St

Independence: Riverview Park, Independence HWY and C St

Klamath Falls: Vets memorial Park, Main & Ewauna Sts

Medford: Veterans Park, I-5 & E Main St

Myrtle Creek: Millside Park

Newport: Donald A Davis Park, Nye beach

Oregon City: Museum of the Ore. Terr., McLaughlin Blvd &
    Tumwater Way

Portland: Washington Park, SW Knights Blvd & SW Zoo Rd

Richland: Post Office Flagpole, Route 86 at 2nd St

Richland: Holcomb Park, Robbinette Rd

Rogue River: Fleming Rest Area, Rogue River Hwy & Depot St

Salem: Restlawn Memorial Gardens, Oak Grove Rd & Wilhelmina-
    Salem Hwy

Springfield: Williamalane Park, Mohawk Blvd & I St

Sutherlin: Central park, Central Ave

The Dalles: Sorosis Park, E Scenic Drive/W Scenic Drive

Pennsylvania:

Allentown: Hamilton & 5th St

Altoona: VA Medical Center, Pleasant Valley Blvd & S 27th St

Beaver: Quay Square, Market St & 3rd St

Bedford: Courthouse Square, W. Penn & S Julianna St

Bristol: Bristol Municipal Building, Bath Rd & Laurel Dr

Bristol: Lions Park, Market St & Samuel Cliff Dr

Butler: Diamond Park, W Diamond & S Cedar Sts

Clarion: S 5th Ave & Grant St

Conshohoken: Vietnam War Memorial Park, Forrest St & W 2nd Ave

Downingtown: Exact location unavailable

Erie: Perry Square, W 6th& Peach Sts

Fredonia: Community Park, Main St at State Route 4024

Harrisburg: State Capitol Memorial Grove, Commonwealth Ave & South St

Lebanon: Veterans Memorial Park, Elm & S 10thSts

Luxor: Twin Lakes Park, Unity Township, off State Route 1049

Macungie: Macungie Memorial Park, Lehigh St & Brookside Rd

Matamoras: 805 Ave N

Pittsburgh: E Carson & S 18thSts

Pittsburgh: North Shore, North Shore Trail & Fort Duquesne Bridge

Philadelphia: Neighborhood Park, Marlborough & E Wildey Sts

Philadelphia: Penn's Landing, I-9f & Spruce St

Tionesta: Foreset County Courthouse, Elm & Davis Sts

Williamsport: W 4th St & Nicely Ln

York: Expo-Fairgrounds, Carlisle Ave & Monarch

Zelienople: Town Park, N Main St & State Route 88

Rhode Island:

Cranston: Cranston High School

Exeter: Veterans Memorial Cemetery, School Land Rd & Dawley Rd

Newport: Courthouse Lawn, Broadway & Bull St

Portsmouth: Portsmouth High School Athletic Field, Patriots Way
& Education Ln

South Carolina:

Anderson: City Park, Standridge Rd & Jackson St
Columbia: Memorial Park, Hampton & Gadsden Sts
Conway: Horry County Courthouse, 3rd Ave & Elm St
Point Pleasant: Naval Support Base, Patriots Point,
Multiple Displays, USS Yorktown State Park
Parris Island: WM Park, De France & Santo Domingo St
Sumter: Civic Plaza, Magnolia & E Canal Sts

South Dakota:

Aberdeen: Anderson Park at Harrison and 7th Avenue SE
Herreid: Herreid High School
Pierre: Adjacent to State Capitol Building, E. Broadway Ave
Sturgis: Veterans Club, Main & Middle Sts

Tennessee:

Clarksville: Public Square, Franklin & N 1st St
Dyersburg: Dyer County Courthouse, W Market St & S Main Ave
Johnson City: Memorial Park, E Main & Bert Sts
Lakeland: Memory Hills Gardens, Cinders & N Germantown Rds
Manchester: Coffee County Courthouse, S Spring & E Fort Sts
Memphis: Thomas & N Watkins Sts
Memphis: West Tennessee Veterans Cemetery, Forest Hill,
Irene Rd & Metcalf Lane
Memphis: Leftwich Tennis Center, Southern Ave & S Goodlett St
Morristown: Hamblen County Courthouse, W 1st N & N Church
Sts
Nashville: Memorial Plaza, Union St & 7th Ave N
Soddy-Daisy: Veterans Park, Dayton Pike & W Walden Circle
Springfield: Robertson County Courthouse, N Main St & E 5th Ave

Texas:

Alice: County Courthouse, Corner of W 3rd& Cameron

Andrews: Veterans Memorial Park, 700 W Broadway

Austin: Texas State Cemetery, E 7th& Comal Sts

Beaumont: 6130 Keith Rd

Big Spring: Veterans Park, Ave. D & 8th St

Blessing: Hawley Cemetery, off County Road 437

Canton: location unknown

Dallas: Fair Park, 1st Ave & Esplanade Pl

Del Rio: Gordon Park, Palm Drive & E Nicholson St

Donna: Old Downtown, N Main St & Hooks Ave

Edgewood: Fair Park

El Paso: City Hall Triangle Park, Myrtle Ave & S Stanton St

Fort Worth: Botanic Garden, Japanese Garden Lane &
    Rock Springs Rd

Galveston: Moody Gardens, Hope Blvd & Lockheed Dr

Houston: Shopping Center, Baneway Drive & Bellaire Blvd

Kaufman: Memorial Park, S Houston St & S Washington St

Lancaster: Heritage Park, N Centre St & E 2nd St

McAllen: Veterans Memorial Park, Galveston Ave & S 29th St

Midland: Midland Airport, Wright Dr & Windecker St

Mineral Wells: Memorial Gardens, S.H. 180 &
    Lake Mineral Wells SH

Mineral Wells: Vietnam War National Museum, Same as above

Odessa: Ector County Courthouse, N Grant Ave & W 4th St

Perryton: Courthouse lawn, SE 5th Ave & Main St

Ranger: Vietnam Veterans Memorial Park, Strawn Rd & Foch St

San Angelo: San Angelo Airport, Knickerbocker Rd & FAA Rd

San Antonio: San Antonio Municipal Auditorium, Navarro &
    E Martin Sts

San Marcos: Veterans Park, 320 Mariposa St (Dunbar Park)

San Marcos: Texas State University, N LBJ Dr& Bobtail Trail

Waco: Brazos River Park, University Park Drive &
    Washington Ave

Utah:

Cedar City: Memorial Park, W 200N & N 100 W

Farmington: Main Courthouse Entrance, State & S Main Sts

Kearns: Veterans Memorial Park, 5400 S & S 4000 W

Mapleton: City Park, E Maple & S Main Sts

Morgan: Morgan County Courthouse, W Young & N State Sts

Murray: Murray City Park, Constitution Circle & E Murray Park

Salt Lake City: State Capitol Grounds, Columbus St & E 300N

Vernal: Uintah County Government Bldg, E Main St & S 100 E

West Valley City: Utah Cultural Celebration Center, W 3100 S

Vermont:

Enosburg Falls: Village Green, Main & Missisquoi Sts

Essex Junction: Memorial Triangle, Main & Pearl Sts

Franklin: N Stanton Rd & Square Rd

Newport: Gardner Park, Gardner Park Rd & SH 5

Rutland: Community Park, S Main St & Spellman Terrace

Sharon: Rest Area I-89 North, Along Vietnam Veterans memorial
Highway North & West of W Hartford.

Waterbury: S Main & Park Sts

Virginia:

Culpeper: Back of the Court House Lawn

Drake's Branch: N Main Street & C.R. 1210

Newport News: Virginia State Monument, Fort Fun &
Kawana Circles

Orange: County Courthouse, W main St & N Madison Rd

Richmond: 621 S Belvedere St

Triangle: Semper Fidelis Memorial Park, I-95 and SH 619

Vienna: Mt Vernon Recreation Center, exact location unknown

Washington:

Forks: City Park, N Forks Ave & Tillicum Lane

Kennewick: Cable Bridge Park, E Columbia Dr & N Gum St

Olympia: Washington State Capitol, SW Angle Dr& 14th Ave SW
Port Townsend: Roadside Park, W Simms Way & Hill St
Richland: Sunset Cemetery, Swift Blvd & Boone Rd
Shelton: W Railroad Ave & N 3rd St
Spokane: Riverfront Park, Inland Northwest Vietnam Veteran
　　Memorial N Washington St
Vancouver: Community Health Center grounds, Plain Blvd & C St
Walla Walla: Fort Walla Walla Park

Washington D.C.:

The Wall, Constitution Gardens, Henry Bacon Dr NW
The Women's Vietnam Memorial, Henry Bacon Dr NW
Vietnam Veterans Memorial Flagpole, Henry Bacon Dr NW

West Virginia:

Bluefield: I-77 Visitors Center, Greasy Ridge Rd & SH 460
Charleston: State Capitol, Greenbrier St & Kanawha Blvd E
Morgantown: War Veterans Memorial Plaza, High & S walnut Sts

Wisconsin:

Arcadia: Memorial Park, Memorial Park Dr
Milwaukee: Milwaukee County Veterans Park, Lincoln Memorial
　　Drive
Neshkoro: S Main & W Wall Streets
Niellsville: The Highground Plaza, Multiple Exhibits, Ridge Rd &
　　SH10
Oshkosh: South Park SH 44 & W 11th Ave
Prescott: Prescott Senior High School, Monroe & St Croix Sts
Sheboygan: veterans Memorial Park, CR TT&22nd St
Sparta: Blyton Park, Cottage St & N Benton St
Two Rivers: Riverview Drive & Terrace Court
Wiota: Former Fort Hamilton, Main & Mineral Sts

Wyoming:

Cheyenne: Municipal Building Courtyard, Pioneer Ave at
W 20th St

Cheyenne: VA Medical Center, on E Pershing Blvd

Cody: Veterans Memorial Park, Greybull Hwy & 26th St

Laramie: UW Campus, E Ivinson Ave & S 9th St

Made in the USA
Charleston, SC
22 February 2016